Babe Ruth

Babe Ruth

Academic Industries, Inc.
West Haven, Connecticut 06516

ISBN 0-88301-792-X

Published by
Academic Industries, Inc.
The Academic Building
Saw Mill Road
West Haven, Connecticut 06516

Printed in the United States of America

Babe Ruth

Contents

BABE RUTH .

The year was 1914. It was the first game of spring train-ing for the Baltimore Orioles. A rookie was batting. He swung. The ball went up . . . and up . . . and out over the fence.

St. Mary's School

It was Babe Ruth's first game as a professional baseball player.

The next day, Ruth woke up early.

What's the matter? What are you doing up?

Just used to it, I guess. We always had to be up early at St. Mary's.

He left the hotel.

Which way to the railroad station?

Right that way, sir.

13

Soon he reached the station.

Do you mind if I watch the trains for a while?

No. Are you catching a train?

Oh, no. I just never saw trains before!

Look at that power!

He was back at the hotel for breakfast.

Is it really true—we order what we want, and the team pays for it?

Yes. But I think they're going to lose money on you!

Babe made friends with the boys who were always around the baseball field.

Will you show me how to pitch with my left arm?

Sure!

You hold the ball like this.

You wind up.

And then you throw.

Now will you let me ride your bike?

Take mine!

No, mine!

One day, when he was riding the bicycle, Babe had an accident.

Wow!

Look out!

Babe put on the brakes and swerved.

Mr. Dunn and Mr. Egan . . . hello!

Jack Dunn was the owner and manager of the Orioles. Egan was the catcher and field captain.

All right, kid! If you want to go back to St. Mary's, keep riding those bicycles!

No, sir! I'll stop right now!

St. Mary's School in Baltimore looked like a prison. George Herman Ruth was sent there when he was about eight years old.

I see you've been sent here because you are "incorrigible." Do you know what that means?

No.

It means you don't obey rules. Here, I am in charge of making people obey.

Gosh!

I think anybody would obey *you*!

Ha-ha! Well, see that you do! Now, come out, and let's play baseball.

Hit some for us, Brother Mathias!

Hit one over the fence!

But in the late afternoon there was an hour or two for games. The favorite game was baseball. The school had forty teams.

Soon George was playing on one of them.

You don't often see a southpaw as catcher!

George is a good one!

Later . . .

George, you're big for your age, and you're a good player. We'll put you on an older boys' team.

That'll be great!

Then there was another change.

We need a pitcher on our best team. Why don't you try it?

Gosh! I don't know how to pitch!

You're big, and you throw hard. I think I can teach you.

Brother Mathias helped George become a good pitcher.

19

POCKET BIOGRAPHIES

When George was nineteen, his team played against Mount St. Joseph's best team. All the boys attended the game.

We won! Twenty-two strikeouts for Ruth! What pitching!

Soon afterward, George was called to the office.

George, this is Mr. Dunn. He owns the Baltimore Orioles.

You did some nice pitching out there!

Thanks.

Mr. Dunn would like you to play for his team next season.

It's a minor league team, but you'll have a chance to move up.

The
Minor
Leagues

It's a great chance, George. Mr. Dunn will pay you $600 for the year. He will become your guardian until you are twenty-one.

That sounds great!

Good! We'll leave soon for spring training camp in North Carolina. I'll see you then!

But do you think I can make it out there?

Sure!

Just after his twentieth birthday, George left St. Mary's. He took his first train ride, to Fayetteville, and followed Jack Dunn onto the field.

Who is that?

Just Dunnie, with his newest babe.

"Babe" was a common baseball word for a rookie. But from then on, George Ruth was known as "Babe."

POCKET BIOGRAPHIES

He had spent most of his life at St. Mary's. He didn't know about trains or hotels or bicycles or money. But he knew about baseball.

In his first game, he hit the ball farther than anyone had ever hit in that park.

The Orioles went on the road. Babe pitched his first full game against the best team in the minor leagues, the Philadelphia Athletics.

That kid's the most promising player I've ever seen!

Finally, spring training ended, and the season began.

Now you will receive $25 a week, and you must pay your bills yourself.

Thanks! I never had more than five dollars at once before!

See that you hold on to it!

Babe hurried to a store.

I want the best you've got!

Certainly, sir!

And then he roared off on a new red motorcycle.

B-r-r-r-OOOOM!

He kept playing well. In May, he got a raise.

I'm going to double your salary, Babe.

And in June he got still another.

Babe, I'm giving you another raise.

Thank you, sir!

But things were not going well for Dunn.

I've given Baltimore a winning team. But the people don't come out to see us play. We're losing money. I have to sell some players.

The Red Sox

On Thursday, July 10, 1914, Dunn told the newspapers of the sale.

Gentlemen, I have sold Ruth, Shore, and Egan to the Boston Red Sox.

On Saturday morning, Babe and the others reached Boston.

First thing, let's check into a hotel.

And second thing, let's eat breakfast!

They went to a coffee shop.

Hello, beautiful! Bring me a double order of eggs.

You must be hungry.

The waitress was Helen Woodford. Soon she and Babe were going out together.

I'm being sent to the Providence minor league team. At the end of the season, though, I'll be back with the Red Sox.

Oh, Babe! I'll miss you!

You won't have a chance. It's only forty miles away.

The Providence Grays were the winners in their league. Babe finished the season with a record of twenty-eight wins and nine losses.

But the season was ending.

I'll be in Baltimore for the winter. It may be April before I see you again!

Look, why don't we get married?

Oh, gosh! I don't know. All right!

They were married at St. Paul's Church, near Baltimore.

Babe was only twenty years old, but already he had a wife, a job in the major leagues, and a good salary.

On May 5, Babe pitched against the New York Yankees.

A home run into the *upper* right stands! Wow!

And hit by a left-handed *pitcher*!

This was Babe's first major league home run.

Then Babe pitched another game. The Red Sox lost.

We lost.

But you did a good job!

Babe's fourth and last home run of the season came in July in St. Louis.

Look at that! Clear out of the park!

It broke a window in a store across the street!

Babe's home run was the longest ball ever hit in the St. Louis park. Babe also hit two doubles and a single, and he pitched a complete game. The Red Sox won, 4-3.

The Red Sox won in their league, but Babe did not get to pitch in the World Series.

I can do it. Just give me a chance!

I know it, Babe. But I want to use right-handed pitchers.

The Red Sox won the World Series. And Babe got a check as a member of the winning team.

That's not bad—$3,780.25! More than my whole salary!

In 1916, Babe had a great season. The fans loved him.

What a guy! Twenty-three wins, nine of them shutouts!

And he hit three home runs in one game!

Once again, the Red Sox were world champions. Babe pitched a fourteen-inning game—the longest ever played in a World Series.

In 1918, the Red Sox got a new manager, Ed Barrow.

You're a star pitcher, Babe, but you're also a great hitter.

Why don't you play outfield on the days you don't pitch?

I think I'll hit even better if I can play every day!

For the next three days, Babe Ruth played at first base or in the outfield. On the fourth day, he pitched ten innings!

This guy's the best! Three home runs in three days, and he's hitting .484!

The fans love it!

That season Babe hit eleven home runs. It was the beginning of a new age in baseball.

The
Yankee
Slugger

In early 1920, Miller Huggins, the manager of the Yankees, came to see Babe.

Hello, Babe. May I talk to you?

Sure. Have I been traded to the Yankees?

That's right—in a deal worth $450,000 to the Red Sox owner.

And we'll double your salary. You'll be making $20,000 a year.

I'll play as hard for the Yankees as I did for the Red Sox!

When the news came out, the Boston fans were angry.

I'll never forgive them for this!

The Red Sox are finished without Babe!

BABE GOES TO YANKEE

Happy New York fans cheered him when he left for the Yankees' spring training camp.

His season didn't start well. But on May 1, he hit his first home run.

Now Babe was famous all over the country. On road trips, there were problems.

At night, Babe would rather go to parties than go to bed.

I've told you before— you can't stay out all night breaking the training rules and still play good baseball!

Sometimes Babe was fined, even suspended. But he never really learned to keep the rules.

With Babe as its star, the Yankees drew large crowds. On April, 18, 1923, the team began playing in a new park.

It's the greatest place I ever saw!

The baseball writers are calling it "The House that Ruth Built!"

Meanwhile, Babe and Helen had separated. In 1923, Babe met Claire Hodgson, and they became friends.

In 1929, Helen died. A few months later, Babe and Claire were married.

It's nice to have someone to talk to.

I'm glad we're friends.

Afterward, they talked to reporters.

Where are you going on your honeymoon?

We're not going on a honeymoon. Babe has baseball games to play!

The next day, the new season opened. Claire went to the game.

Babe hit a home run, and he blew a kiss to Claire as he passed third base.

Claire had a daughter, Julia, by an earlier marriage. Babe had an adopted daughter, Dorothy. Now the families lived together.

Babe liked children. They were his favorite fans.

Sign my card, Babe!

You big boys give the little ones a chance!

Sometimes, driving home after a game, Babe would see boys playing ball.

Hey, look! It's Babe Ruth!

Come and hit a few with us, Babe!

Often he would stop and play with them.

Now back up and catch this pop fly!

Babe also spent much time visiting children who were in the hospital.

Now, you hold the bat like this. And when you're a little stronger, you can swing it!

From 1926 through 1932, Babe Ruth averaged fifty home runs a year. He batted .354, and played in seven World Series.

The Yankees did it again!

That Babe! Can you believe he's thirty-seven years old?

He held or shared sixty-one baseball records. Twenty-eight were World Series records. And his lifetime home run record—714—would not be broken for forty years!

Babe stopped playing in 1935. But twelve years later he had not been forgotten.

Did you see this? Babe Ruth is in the hospital!

Gosh! I wish I could see him play baseball!

These are letters for Babe Ruth. And there are more outside!

Thirty thousand letters arrived. And when he left the hospital, Babe needed help from the police to get to his car.

Get well quick!

Later, a day was set aside to honor Babe.

Sunday, April 27, will be Babe Ruth Day all over the major leagues!

In New York, too?

At Yankee Stadium. They want me to come!

Sixty thousand other people were there as well.

And now, ladies and gentlemen . . . Babe Ruth!

Thank you, ladies and gentlemen.

There have been so many lovely things said about me. I'm glad I have this chance to thank everybody.

On August 16, 1948, Babe Ruth died. His body was brought to Yankee Stadium where his fans came to see him for the last time.

People came—77,000 of them—to say goodbye. No one would ever forget the thrills he had given them during his life.

THE END

Do you remember?

Babe was only eight when he was sent to St. Mary's School. His teacher saw that he was:

a. a good student.   b. a tall boy.
                    c. a good baseball player.

With the Boston Orioles he played:

a. pitcher.   b. first base.   c. outfielder.

POCKET BIOGRAPHIES

Babe Ruth held a record forty years. It was for:

a. the greatest number of home runs in a single career.
b. the most strikeouts in a pitching career.
c. the most walks.

Yankee Stadium was also known as:

a. "The House that Ruth Built."
b. Disneyland.
c. the Olympic Stadium.

Quiz
Yourself

(Answers at end of section)

Words to know

salary	money one receives for doing a job
guardian	one who takes care of another person
World Series	games played between the winners of both leagues to decide the world champion team
inning	the time it takes for each team to make three outs in a baseball game
reporters	people who write stories for newspapers

BABE RUTH

Can you use them?

Using the words above, complete the following sentences.

1. A child whose parents have died would be looked after by a
   _____ .

2. In 1978, the Yankees won the _____ .

3. Some sports _____ like to write about the personal lives of athletes.

4. When a person is given extra work to do, he usually receives an increase in his _____ .

5. At the end of the third _____ , the score was tied.

Using pictures

In reading illustrated stories, you will find it helpful to "read" the pictures as well as the words. Look at this picture. It shows the Red Sox manager asking Babe Ruth to play outfield on days when he wasn't pitching. Babe was such a good baseball player that people expected more of him than they did of other players. Look at pages 21 and 27 to see some of the things Babe did that made the fans like him so much.

While you are reading

Because he was a star, Babe Ruth had many problems that ordinary people never have. Some of Babe's own qualities caused him problems, too. While you are reading, make a list of all the problems Babe Ruth had to face because of his fame or because of the kind of person he was.

_____

_____

_____

_____

How well did you read?

When you have finished reading, answer the following questions.

1. Who gave Babe Ruth his first chance to play baseball for a major league team?

    (Check the correct answer.)

    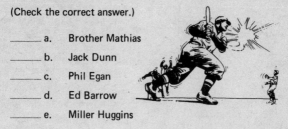

    _____ a.   Brother Mathias

    _____ b.   Jack Dunn

    _____ c.   Phil Egan

    _____ d.   Ed Barrow

    _____ e.   Miller Huggins

2. Why was Babe Ruth sold by the Orioles to the Boston Red Sox?

    (Check the correct answer.)

    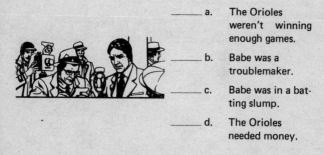

    _____ a.   The Orioles weren't winning enough games.

    _____ b.   Babe was a troublemaker.

    _____ c.   Babe was in a batting slump.

    _____ d.   The Orioles needed money.

3. What did Babe do with his first paycheck?

    (Check the correct answer.)

    _____ a. He used the money to buy a motorcycle.

    _____ b. He sent the money to his wife.

    _____ c. He put the check in the bank.

    _____ d. He donated the money to St. Mary's School.

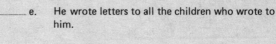

4. How did Babe show his thanks to the young fans who always came to see him?

    (Check the correct *answers.*)

    _____ a. He always signed their scorecards when they asked.

    _____ b. He gave them money to fix up their baseball fields.

    _____ c. He often stopped to play ball with them.

    _____ d. He visited them in the hospitals when they were sick.

    _____ e. He wrote letters to all the children who wrote to him.

5. How did George Herman Ruth come to be called "Babe"?
   (Check the correct answer.)

   _____ a. George never really grew up.

   _____ b. His teammates at St. Mary's
   used the name to make fun
   of George.

   _____ c. George always liked children
   better than he liked adults.

   _____ d. The Orioles' players used the
   name because it meant "rookie."

Using what you've read

   During his life, Babe Ruth was often the subject of newspaper
articles. People loved to read and to talk about him. Suppose that
you had been a newspaper reporter during Babe Ruth's time. What
questions would you have asked Babe about his career in the major
leagues? How do you think he would have answered your questions? Write a brief account of your interview, using the form below. Include at least three questions and answers.

Question:

Answer:

ANSWER KEY

BABE RUTH

Can you use them?

1.	guardian	3.	reporters
2.	World Series	4.	salary
	5. inning		

How well did you read?

1.	b	3.	a
2.	d	4.	a, c, d
	5. d		

NOTES

NOTES

NOTES

NOTES

COMPLETE LIST OF POCKET CLASSICS AVAILABLE

CLASSICS

C 1 Black Beauty
C 2 The Call of the Wild
C 3 Dr. Jekyll and Mr. Hyde
C 4 Dracula
C 5 Frankenstein
C 6 Huckleberry Finn
C 7 Moby Dick
C 8 The Red Badge of Courage
C 9 The Time Machine
C10 Tom Sawyer
C11 Treasure Island
C12 20,000 Leagues Under the Sea
C13 The Great Adventures of Sherlock Holmes
C14 Gulliver's Travels
C15 The Hunchback of Notre Dame
C16 The Invisible Man
C17 Journey to the Center of the Earth
C18 Kidnapped
C19 The Mysterious Island
C20 The Scarlet Letter
C21 The Story of My Life
C22 A Tale of Two Cities
C23 The Three Musketeers
C24 The War of the Worlds
C25 Around the World in Eighty Days
C26 Captains Courageous
C27 A Connecticut Yankee in King Arthur's Court
C28 The Hound of the Baskervilles
C29 The House of the Seven Gables
C30 Jane Eyre

COMPLETE LIST OF POCKET CLASSICS AVAILABLE
(cont'd)

COMPLETE LIST OF POCKET CLASSICS AVAILABLE
(cont'd)

SHAKESPEARE

S 1 As You Like It
S 2 Hamlet
S 3 Julius Caesar
S 4 King Lear
S 5 Macbeth
S 6 The Merchant of Venice
S 7 A Midsummer Night's Dream
S 8 Othello
S 9 Romeo and Juliet
S10 The Taming of the Shrew
S11 The Tempest
S12 Twelfth Night

BIOGRAPHIES

B 1 Charles Lindbergh
B 2 Amelia Earhart
B 3 Houdini
B 4 Walt Disney
B 5 Davy Crockett
B 6 Daniel Boone
B 7 Elvis Presley
B 8 The Beatles
B 9 Benjamin Franklin
B10 Martin Luther King, Jr.
B11 Abraham Lincoln
B12 Franklin D. Roosevelt
B13 George Washington
B14 Thomas Jefferson
B15 Madame Curie
B16 Albert Einstein
B17 Thomas Edison
B18 Alexander Graham Bell
B19 Vince Lombardi
B20 Pelé
B21 Babe Ruth
B22 Jackie Robinson
B23 Jim Thorpe
B24 Althea Gibson

S0-BCZ-837

C I T Y P A C K
Tokyo

By Martin Gostelow

Fodor's

Fodor's Travel Publications
New York • Toronto • London • Sydney • Auckland

WWW.FODORS.COM

Contents

About this book

KEY TO SYMBOLS

✚ Map reference to the location on the fold-out map accompanying this book

✉ Address

☎ Telephone number

🕐 Opening times

🍴 Restaurant or café on premises or nearby

Ⓜ Nearest subway station

🚉 Nearest train station

🚌 Nearest bus route

⛴ Nearest riverboat or ferry stop

♿ Facilities for visitors with disabilities

✋ Admission charge

↔ Other nearby places of interest

❓ Tours, lectures, or special events

► Indicates the page where you will find a fuller description

ℹ Tourist information

Citypack Tokyo's six sections cover the six most important aspects of your visit to Tokyo:

- An overview of the city and its people
- Itineraries, walks, and excursions
- The top 25 sights to visit
- Features about different aspects of the city that make it special
- Detailed listings of restaurants, hotels, stores, and nightlife
- Practical information

In addition, text boxes provide fascinating extra facts and snippets, highlights of places to visit, and invaluable practical advice.

CROSS-REFERENCES

To help you make the most of your visit, cross-references, indicated by ► , show you where to find additional information about a place or subject.

MAPS

The fold-out map in the wallet at the back of the book is a comprehensive street plan of Tokyo. All the map references given in the book refer to this map. For example, the Japanese Sword Museum in Yoyogi, Shibuya-ku, has the following information: ✚ C5—indicating the grid square of the map in which the Japanese Sword Museum will be found.

The downtown maps found on the inside front and back covers of the book itself are for quick reference. They show the Top 25 Sights, described on pages 26–50, which are clearly plotted by number (**1** – **25**, not page number) from west to east.

ADMISSION CHARGES

An indication of the admission charge for sights is given by categorizing the standard adult rate as follows: ✋ expensive (more than ¥1,000), ✋ moderate (¥600–1,000), and ✋ inexpensive (under ¥600).

TOKYO *life*

INTRODUCING TOKYO

Salaryman

He's the man in the dark suit and white shirt, seen on the subway or hurrying to the office, where he'll work until 7PM and then go to a bar to unwind, still with the people he's been with all day. They will drink, smoke, and snack, and may not get home until after midnight. Salaryman joined the company straight from college and hopes to spend his career climbing the corporate ladder, although the old idea of a job for life is fading fast. Although still typical, recession is greatly changing working patterns in Japan.

A Japanese tradition, the tea ceremony

At first sight, this megapolis looks discouragingly gray and monotonous, but it soon comes into focus as self-contained districts that are like separate towns and villages, each with its own flavor. Most areas have their followings and once you learn to use the superb subway system, you'll find Tokyo's many districts within minutes of each other. Upmarket, glitzy Ginza attracts tourists and the wealthy, while Asakusa, with its Sensoji temple, is the spiritual home of older locals, and where some 30 million visitors flock every year. Excellent budget shopping is available around Ueno, in the north, although most districts have a number of department stores. Meanwhile the young will be seriously relaxing at busy Shibuya or Ikebukuro, or strolling tree-lined Dogonzaka on a shopping expedition towards the trendy Aoyama 1-Chome district. Others may prefer the fleshpots of Shinjuku. Homesick travelers often head for Roppongi, where expats go for a lively night out.

The massive 1923 Kanto earthquake and the World War II fire bombing destroyed large parts of Tokyo and left much of the city in ruins. As a result old and historical buildings are few and far between. However, there is a great deal of sylish modern architecture, and small charming corners turn up here and there: an exquisite art collection on the top floor of an anonymous office tower; a tranquil shrine in the shadow of an elevated expressway. Even in the hectic city, you are aware of the seasons: winter's frosts, spring blossoms, and the gold of fall leaves. And while you'll occasionally see older women dressed in kimonos, most Tokyoites are slavish followers of Western fashions.

Shinjuku at night

People take care of their own space, and the infinitely courteous local police look after their own little neighborhoods, on foot or bicycle or on duty in a roadside hut. People here are constantly on the move, but the crowds are managed with remarkable efficiency; patience and self-control are instilled from birth and reinforced by example. The population is the least mixed of any great city.

After dark, countless elaborate neon advertising billboards transform Tokyo. One hundred thousand restaurants and drinking dens beckon with flashing signs and glowing lanterns. In spite of years of recession, there still seems to be money for leisure and Tokyoites, especially the younger generation, know how to enjoy it. After the long day, office workers like to let off steam together over a few beers or whiskies. Salaryman and boss sing songs in a karaoke bar or even talk frankly. Toward midnight, the entertainment districts are full of cheerful revelers heading for the last train home to sleep it off before the work day begins again.

OL

A woman is often not expected to have a career. To fill in the years until she gets married, she might work as an *oeru* (office lady or OL—pronounced o-eru). Men take the "real" jobs: the *oeru* shuffles paper, pours tea, and looks pretty. But she exacts a sort of revenge: a young salaryman has to spend his spare money socializing with colleagues, while, in spite of her lower pay, the *oeru* can afford to take foreign vacations. Her horizons may become so wide that her male counterpart seems gauche and inexperienced by comparison.

7

PEOPLE & EVENTS FROM HISTORY

Emperor Hirohito

IEYASU TOKUGAWA (1542–1616)

As a child, the future ruler spent years as a hostage in the courts of rival clans. He grew up into a cunning, watchful, and ruthless leader. After the death of Hideyoshi in 1598, Ieyasu was sworn—as a member of the regency council —to support the succession of Hideyoshi's young son, but mutual suspicion among the regents soon led to war. Ieyasu's forces were victorious at the battle of Sekigahara in 1600, taking the title of *shogun* in 1603. His stronghold, Edo (later renamed Tokyo), became the capital, and the Tokugawa dynasty ruled Japan until 1867.

EMPEROR HIROHITO (1901–89)

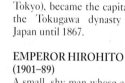

A small, shy man whose appearance and manner belied the divine status accorded to him by tradition, Hirohito traveled widely in his youth and admired Western ways. But as emperor he remained passive as Japan's military leaders took the road to war. He spoke only vaguely to his ministers and never in public. Until 1945, when he called on Japan, in a radio broadcast, to "endure the unendurable" and surrender to the Allies. This was the first time that most of his subjects had ever heard his voice.

GENERAL DOUGLAS MACARTHUR (1880–1964)

As Supreme Commander in Japan from 1945 to 1951, the charismatic, often controversial American, had absolute power, more than any ruler since the *shogun*s. Paradoxically, he used it to build a democracy. Taking over a starving wasteland, he rejected calls for the trial or removal of Hirohito and gained the confidence and co-operation of the Japanese people. His dismissal over the conduct of the Korean War caused widespread shock in Japan.

The pilot and the *shogun*

In April 1600, the lone surviving ship of a Dutch trading fleet reached Japan, sailed by a mere six men. One was an English pilot, Will Adams. He was taken to meet Ieyasu, who was eager to learn about European ways and who asked Adams to build him a ship. The pilot ("*Anjin-san*") spent the rest of his life serving the *shogun*s, dying in 1620. Readers of James Clavell's novel *Shogun* will recognize the story, although he changed names and invented many details.

CONTEMPORARY TOKYOITES

SHIGEO NAGASHIMA (b. 1936)

A much-loved national sports hero and figure, Nagashima was a star batter with Tokyo's Giants baseball team and later their manager until he retired to become a TV commentator. He had been on the sidelines 12 years when the Giants hit a bad patch of form and he was brought back in 1993, at the age of 56, to restore their fortunes. It worked. In the first year, they placed second in their league; the following season they took the league championship and went on to win the Japan Series finals as well.

KENZABURO OE (b. 1935)

This prolific novelist was awarded the Nobel Prize for Literature in 1994, causing a run on his books in Japan where they had not been widely read before. Many of his compatriots find his interweaving of political themes and fantasy "difficult." He says his work has less to do with Japanese literary traditions than to European thought as embodied by William Blake and James Joyce. Oe's son, severely disabled as a baby, seemed to respond only to sound; Oe played recorded bird songs to stimulate his son, who grew up to be a noted composer.

*The novelist
Kenzaburo Oe*

YOTARO KOBAYASHI (b. 1933)

The conservative economist and Fuji-Xerox president is one of the leading figures in the Keidanren. This influential organization of business chiefs had previously always been dominated by the bosses of the great *zaibatsu*, the heavy industry-banking conglomerates.

MAKIKO TANAKA (b. 1944)

The tough and outspoken daughter of former Liberal Democratic Party prime minister Kakuei Tanaka served as Minister of Science in the 1994 Murayama government. Steeped in politics from birth, she overcame her father's opposition and studied in the United States, becoming an accomplished speaker who says what she thinks—a quality almost unheard-of in Japanese women. Now a senator, she is spoken of as a possible future prime minister.

Woman in orbit

Former science minister Makiko Tanaka's talk with Chiaki Mukai, the first Japanese woman astronaut, during the 15 days she spent orbiting in a US Space shuttle in 1994, represented twin pinnacles of achievement for Japanese womanhood. A heart surgeon, Mukai is a heroine to many women who feel that they have not been able to realize their own potential. She is "more like a man," they say.

9

A CHRONOLOGY

10,000–300 BC	Jomon Period. Neolithic hunting and fishing culture; decorative pottery making.
300 BC–AD 250	Yayoi Period. Immigrants from Asia introduce metal working and rice-paddy cultivation.
250–710	Kofun Culture. From 300 to 400 gradual unification under Yamato clan, whose leader takes title of emperor. Yamato power declines 400–600. Growing influence of Chinese culture, and rapid spread of Buddhism.
794	Imperial capital moves from Nara to Kyoto.
850–1150	Advisors to the emperor acquire more and more power. Rise of the *samurai* (warrior) class.
1192	Minamoto are victorious in a power struggle. Yoritomo Minamoto rules from Kamakura as *shogun* or warlord. The emperor in Kyoto becomes a virtual puppet.
12th–16th centuries	Frequent civil wars between rival clans.
1274 and 1281	Mongol invasion fleets destroyed by typhoons (*kamikaze* or "divine wind").
1336	Ashikaga Takauji takes over as *shogun* and establishes his rule in Kyoto.
1543	A Portuguese ship makes the first landfall by Europeans on the coast of Japan.
1572–1600	The warlord Nobunaga Oda seizes power in Kyoto. After his murder in 1582, Hideyoshi Toyotomi unites the whole country. On Hideyoshi's death (1598), a power struggle ensues between regional warlords.
1600–39	Ieyasu Tokugawa is victorious at the battle of Sekigahara (➤ 8). The Tokugawa shogunate is established (1603), with its capital at Edo (the future Tokyo). A long period of isolation from the outside world begins.
1840s	Foreign countries press Japan to open its ports.

1853 and 1858	A U.S. fleet under Commodore Matthew Perry anchors in Tokyo Bay. Treaty of Kanagawa (now Yokohama) signed in 1858 opens ports to trade.
1867–68	Supporters of 15-year-old Emperor Meiji launch a *coup d'état* against the shogunate. Edo is renamed Tokyo ("Eastern Capital"). Shinto is declared the state religion.
1894–1910	War with China (1894–95) and Russia (1904–05). In 1910 Japan annexes Korea.
1923	A devasting earthquake in the city kills about 140,000.
1926	Hirohito becomes emperor.
1930s	Government is increasingly dominated by military leadership. Japan invades China (1937).
1940–45	Economic sanctions imposed on Japan (1940). In 1941 Japan attacks Pearl Harbor and U.S.A. enters World War II. Defeat by the U.S. navy in the battle of Midway marks the turning point of the war. In 1945 massive air raids destroy much of Tokyo. Atomic bombs are dropped on Hiroshima and Nagasaki. Japan surrenders.
1945–1952	U.S. General Douglas MacArthur rules as benevolent dictator. Emperor Hirohito renounces claim to divine status. Japanese independence restored in 1952.
1960s	Rapid economic and industrial recovery. Tokyo hosts Olympic Games in 1964.
1980s	Japan becomes the world's greatest trading nation. Tokyo's stock market booms. Emperor Akihito succeeds Hirohito in 1989.
1991–94	Recession. Stock market falls by 60 percent.
1995	Earthquake destroys much of Kobe.
2000	Amid record unemployment and bankruptcies, the economy begins a slow recovery.

11

TOKYO IN FIGURES

Geography
- Latitude and longitude: 35° 41' N, 139° 41' E. Tokyo is farther south than Sicily, level with central California.
- Altitude: sea level to 200 feet.
- Distance from New York: 6,200 miles.
- Distance from San Francisco: 5,135 miles.
- Distance from London: 6,725 miles.
- Distance from Sydney: 4,850 miles.
- Area: 783 sq.mi. in greater metropolitan area, 226 sq.mi. in the inner metropolitan area. The latter is made up of 23 wards, some of them big cities in their own right.
- Population: 8,000,000 in the inner metropolitan area; 12,500,000 in the greater metropolitan area.

Finance
- Annual budget of the Tokyo prefecture government: ¥6,000,000,000,000 ($56 billion, £37 billion).
- Property values: Up to $60,000 per sq.yd.

People
- Five million people travel to work.
- Typical commute: An hour's ride is typical, two hours not unusual; at least half of all commuters appear to be asleep.
- Motor vehicles: 5 million in the city, 2 million in use on any given day.
- TV watched: Average of 26 hours per week.
- Main extracurricular activity for school-children: Extra classes.
- Literacy: 99.7 percent.
- Life expectancy: 84 for women; 77 for men (among the world's highest).
- Restaurants per capita: more than anywhere in the world.
- Percentage of men say they get drunk at least one night a week: 75 percent.

Worried Toyko
- Percentage of Tokyoites who worry about their standard of living: 90 percent.
- Percentage of Tokyoites who worry about being replaced by computers and robots: 74 percent.
- Percentage of Tokyoites who worry that there may be a major earthquake soon: 80 percent.

TOKYO
how to organize your time

ITINERARIES

After a quick look around the district where you are staying, make learning how to use the subway a top priority (➤ 90). It's best to take in as many sights as you are interested in at any one location to save backtracking. Note that most museums, some gardens, and other attractions close on Mondays.

ITINERARY ONE	PALACE GARDENS & GINZA
Morning	Start where it all began, the site of the first Tokugawa *shogun*'s mighty Edo Castle, on a low hill in the Imperial Palace East Garden (➤ 36). Walk along the moat to Hibiya Park (➤ 40), then dive into the famous shopping and entertainment district of Ginza (➤ 41).
Lunch	Grab a bite in one of Ginza's restaurants or department stores—you'll find all tastes catered for.
Afternoon	The fine Bridgestone Museum of Art (➤ 52), the Idemitsu Museum of Arts (➤ 52), and the famous Kabuki-za Theater (➤ 78) are a short walk away.
Evening	You could spend a fortune on dining out in Ginza, but you don't have to: there are reasonably priced restaurants, too.
ITINERARY TWO	TSUKIJI & ASAKUSA
Morning	Get up at around 4.30PM (jetlag might make it easier) and go to the fish market at Tsukiji (➤ 44). Have a sushi breakfast in the market. Take the Sumida river cruise to Asakusa (➤ 49) from the Hama Rikyu Garden (➤ 43) nearby.
Lunch	There's a variety of options at Asakusa with the emphasis on Japanese and Asian cuisine.
Afternoon	Combine Asakusa and Ueno Park (➤ 17), with its museums and shrines—three stops on the subway.
Evening	Spend the evening dining and possibly check-ing out the nightlife in Roppongi (➤ 80).

ITINERARY THREE	SHINJUKU & HARAJUKU
Morning	You are bound to pass through the vast, frenetic Shinjuku Station (► 27) more than once during your Tokyo visit. Stop off and take the west exit, which leads to the city's biggest camera stores. Continue on to the futuristic Metropolitan Government Offices (► 26) for fine views from the observatory on the 45th floor.
Lunch	Return to the station—lunch options galore.
Afternoon	Lively, young Harajuku (► 31) is a starting point for visits to the Meiji Shrine (► 30), Ota Museum (► 53). Stroll down the Omotesando-dori, a mecca of shops, cafés, and restaurants . This is one of Tokyo's most pleasant locales and where you can find many elegant, expensive boutiques.
Evening	Check out the vibrant nightlife among the narrow streets of Kabukicho (► 80) east of Shinjuku Station.

ITINERARY FOUR	LOOSE ENDS
Morning	Use the subway system to get around to places you have missed. Visit the controversial Yasukuni Shrine (► 38). Look at the view from Tokyo Tower (► 34), and take in nearby Zojoji Temple (► 35). Marvel at *samurai* values at Sengakuji Temple (► 33).
Lunch	Drop into any convenient noodle bar.
Afternoon	Tokyo Disneyland (► 50) is fun—not only for children—and only 15 minutes by train from Tokyo Station.
Evening	With its restaurants, beer hall, and music bars the Shibuya after-dark scene is more lively than Ginza, more Japanese than Roppongi Garden Place at Ebisu (► 32). Reached via a moving footway from the JR Ebisu station, it is well worth a visit.

WALKS

THE SIGHTS

INFORMATION

Distance 4 miles

Time 2 ½ hours

Start point Asakusa river bus pier

🚇 N2

🚤 Asakusa pier, from Hama Rikyu Garden (▶ 43)

Ⓜ Asakusa (Ginza and Asakusa lines)

End point Inaricho subway station

🚇 B10

Ⓜ Inaricho (Ginza line), or continue walking along Asakusa-dori to Ueno (▶ 17)

Sumida River and the Asahi Brewery (right)

A WALK AROUND ASAKUSA & KAPPABASHI

At the river bus pier or the exit from Asakusa subway station, look across the Sumida River at the dramatic Asahi Brewery buildings designed by Philippe Starck in 1989.

Two blocks west of the river is Kaminarimon, one of the gates to Sensoji (or Asakusa Kannon) Temple. Through it is the pedestrian Nakamise-dori, a street lined with small shops. Take note of the street to the left, Denboin-dori, before touring the temple. Return to Denboin-dori, which leads to the entertainment district, with theaters and places to eat. The Nakase restaurant (▶ 65), on the first corner, is noted for tempura. Many inexpensive noodle shops are on the side streets. Hanayashiki, behind the temple, is a children's amusement park.

Cut through to the west to the Asakusa View tower on the broad Kokusai-dori. Turn left and follow Kokusai-dori for one block and then turn right onto Asakusa-dori for 300 yards, past two temples, to meet the main street of Kappabashi, famous for its shops selling kitchen supplies, including the plastic replica food that restaurants display in their windows to show what they serve. Turn left (south) and continue to Asakusa-dori, marked by a giant chef's head. A right turn leads to Inaricho subway station.

A WALK AROUND UENO & YANAKA

Ueno is one of the city's busiest hubs. The east exit from Ueno's JR station leads to Showa-dori, in the shadow of an elevated expressway. Turn left (north) and you will quickly be in so-called "motorcycle heaven" (➤ 72). Retrace your steps to the main road junction south of the station and look for the archway leading to Ameyoko, one of Tokyo's liveliest markets, with thousands of stands stretching as far as Okachimachi JR Station. At the market's Ueno end, cross Chuo-dori and enter Ueno Park at its southeast corner, where the Shitamachi folk museum faces Shinobazu Pond, filled with waterfowl. There is more to see in the park, including many shrines and museums and a zoo featuring giant pandas (➤ 62).

Yanaka bric-a-brac shop

North of Ueno Park, west of the railroad, is Yanaka, whose narrow streets and old shops and houses escaped both the 1923 earthquake and 1945 bombing. With its dozens of temples and gardens, this is more like Kyoto than Tokyo. You may well get lost, but it doesn't matter as you will

eventually bump into either the Yanaka cemetery (north of Tokyo Museum) on the area's eastern end or Nippori JR Station to the north, and you can get your bearings. Finish at Nezu subway station on the western edge of Yanaka.

A traditional house in Yanaka

THE SIGHTS

- Ameyoko market (➤ 72)
- Ueno Park (➤ 59)
- Shitamachi Museum (➤ 54)
- Tokyo National Museum (➤ 46)
- Yanaka streets and houses
- Yanaka cemetery

INFORMATION

Distance 5 miles
Time 2 ½ hours
Start point Ueno JR Station
✚ L2
🚉 Ueno (Yamanote Line)
🚇 Ueno (Ginza Line)
End point Nezu subway station
✚ K1
🚉 Nezu
Note: Museums in Ueno Park close Mon (or Tue if Mon is a national holiday)

17

EVENING STROLLS

INFORMATION

Ginza
Distance 1 mile
Time 1½ hours
Start point Higashi-Ginza subway station

✚ K7
🚇 Higashi-Ginza
End point Yurakucho station

✚ K6
🚇 Yurakucho
🚉 Yurakucho

In the early evening, many stores are still open and people pack into bars and restaurants; around 11PM they all pour out again.

Shinjuku-Kabukicho
Distance 1 mile
Time 1½ hours
Start and end point Shinjuku Station (east exit)

✚ D4
🚇 Shinjuku
🚉 Shinjuku

Early in the evening, people stroll about, deciding where to go. Later, the usually amiable crowd reels its way home.

A traditional orchestra plays for kabuki theater

AROUND GINZA

At Higashi-Ginza station, take a look at the traditional Kabuki-za Theater (➤ 78) before heading up Harumi-dori toward the brightly lighted main Ginza crossing with Chuo-dori lined with some of Tokyo's biggest stores, which stay open—and busy—until around 8PM; off the avenue explore the grid of narrow side streets. The price of area real estate means that no site is wasted. Finish your walk back on Harumi-dori and take the subway at Ginza, or continue to Yurakucho where there are reasonably priced places to eat near the station and under the tracks.

AROUND SHINJUKU-KABUKICHO

Tokyo's most varied entertainment district, with practically no street crime, starts just east of Shinjuku station (subway or JR). Follow signs to Kabukicho; if you don't see one, turn left towards the Shinjuku Prince tower, the red brick hotel rising above the Shinjuku terminus. Spread out to the right of it is a maze of narrow streets lined by bars, strip joints, massage parlors, and superb ethnic restaurants. If you go through the doors of any establishment, ask the price first—of everything—or you could be in for a shock. The big Koma theater, a famous theater with a revolving stage but with no performances in English, is a landmark. North and east of it things get raunchier, and then peter out into anonymity. Turn back and, if lost, ask for *Shinjuku eki* (station).

ORGANIZED SIGHTSEEING

Sightseeing tours are somewhat expensive—roughly ¥5,000 for a half-day, ¥12,000 for a full day with lunch, ¥13,000 for a night tour with dinner—but they'll save your shoe leather. Tour companies pick up only from the main hotels and leave all participants in the Ginza area at the tour's end. You can check on tour options and prices at the TIC (➤ 91) or at hotel desks. Tour companies inlcude Japan Gray Line Co. Ltd ✉ 3-3-3 Nishi-Shinbashi, Minato-ku ☎ 3433–5745 and Sunrise Tours, Japan Travel Bureau Incorporated ✉ 2–3–11 Higashishinagawa, Shinagawa-ku ☎ 55796–5454.

The Ginza district

CITY TOURS

Typical tours of the city's sights include the Imperial Palace East Garden, Meiji Shrine, Tokyo Tower, and Asakusa, (sometimes reached by the Sumida river bus); the level of traffic makes the time you have at the various stops unpredictable. Morning and afternoon tours are offered, as well as all-day packages including lunch. Some tours include demonstrations of Japanese flower-arranging, doll-making, or a tea ceremony. An Industrial Tokyo tour may take you to Japan Airlines maintenance base at Haneda Airport, the Kirin Brewery, or the Isuzu car factory. Skip the tour to Tokyo Disneyland (➤ 50), which gives you seven hours in the park and unlimited rides—you can easily do this on your own.

OUT-OF-TOWN TOURS

Excursions are available to Kamakura (➤ 20), Hakone (➤ 21), Mount Fuji (➤ 21), and Nikko with its famous Kegon Falls. Skip the single-day Kamakura–Hakone trips; they are too rushed. There are one- and two-day tours to Kyoto (➤ 22–23); you can make these part of a combination vacation of any desired length.

Tokyo by night

The widely advertised evening tours generally combine dinner with a show. You have a choice of menus, perhaps sukiyaki, *kushiage* (➤ 64), or steak, and of entertainment. Some tours offer a chance to sample *kabuki* theater (➤ 78) and traditional *geisha* entertainment of music, song, and conversation—true *geishas* don't speak English. Hato Tours offers a Helicopter Night Cruise tour. The 4-hour tour includes a 10-minute helicopter ride over the city and an Indian meal. It costs ¥18,900, which includes transfers to and from your hotel. ☎ 3435–6081 for reservations.

19

EXCURSIONS

INFORMATION

Kamakura

Distance 30 miles

Time About 1 hour from Tokyo

🎫 Sites vary. Typically: Mar–Sep daily 8–5. Oct–Feb daily 8–4

🍴 Around Kamakura Station and along Wakamiya Avenue

🚆 Kita-kamakura or Kamakura from Tokyo Station, lower level Track 1 (JR Yokosuka Line), or at intermediate stops, Shinbashi or Shinagawa. Hase by local train from Kamakura

♿ Few (difficult access, hilly sites)

💴 Moderate

❓ Day tours from Tokyo only visit major sites. Area is well signposted in English. The Kamakura Information Center at Kamakura Station sells maps of the area

KAMAKURA

Tokyo seems far away as the train passes through the wooded slopes that surround the seaside town of Kamakura on three sides. The military ruler Minamoto Yoritomo set up his base here in 1192, leaving the emperor as a figurehead in Kyoto, and Kamakura remained the seat of power until 1333. Its many shrines and temples are spread out, but you can use the railroad to cut down the amount of walking. In summer, the beach, 15 minutes walk from the station, is popular.

Near Hase Station The Great Buddha (*Daibutsu*) at Kotokuin Temple is second in size to Nara's, but is a finer sculpture. Cast in bronze in 1252, the 37-foot statue is hollow; you can climb inside. Hasedera Temple on a nearby hillside houses a 30-foot-high wooden carving of Kannon, said to have been washed ashore over 1,000 years ago. Infinitely touching are the countless tiny images of Jizo similar to those found at the Zojoji Temple (► 35).

Near Kamakura Station The wide Wakamiya ("Young Prince") Avenue leads from the sea to Hachimangu Shrine, by way of the steep Drum Bridge. Near the shrine, Kamakura Museum houses relics of the era of its glory and some fine woodblock prints (► 53).

Near Kita-kamakura Station 13th-century Engakuji Temple is one of the most important Zen Buddhist temples in Japan. The neighboring Tokeiji Temple was once the only refuge for women fleeing cruel husbands.

The Hachimangu Shrine

HAKONE

The mountainous area west of Tokyo, with lakes and countless hot springs, is a favorite weekend target of local day-trippers. Visit mid-week to avoid peak vacation times (► 24, 89). From Hakone-Yumoto, the Hakone Tozan Railroad zigzags over the mountains, making stops on the way. Miyanoshita is a resort with thermal pools and moutain walks. Stop for lunch or tea at the historic Fujiya Hotel. Next to Chokoku-no-Mori Station is Hakone Open Air Museum, with a spectacular sculpture garden and gallery. From the last station, Gora, a cable car soars over Owakudani valley, where sulfurous fumes and smoke pour from a dozen crevices. Stop here and buy eggs boiled in the hot springs. Another 25 minutes by cable car takes you to Togendai, the base for cruises on Lake Ashi.

MOUNT FUJI (FUJI-YAMA)

For most visitors, a view of the perfect volcanic cone is enough, especially as reflected in Lake Ashi. If you want to see it close up, head for Kawaguchiko, four miles away. Gogome, closer still, is the main starting point for people making the 4- to 5-hour trip to the 12,388-foot summit. The season is short (July 1 to August 31) and weather can be bad, so be prepared with warm clothing. Always check the weather conditions (see panel) before making an ascent.

INFORMATION

Hakone
Distance 56 miles
Time 1½ hours from Tokyo, then 55 minutes on local train
🎨 Open Air Museum: Mar–Oct: daily 9–5. Nov–Feb: 9–4
🍴 At and near stations
🚉 Hakone-Yumote (Limited Express from Shinjuku Station, Odakyu Line)
♿ Good 💰 Expensive
❓ On Hakone Tozan Railroad, a "Hakone Free Pass" (not free) covers 4 days' travel by trains, buses, cable car, boats
Mount Fuji
Distance 60 miles
Time 2 hours from Tokyo
☎ English language information line/weather: 0555 23 3000
🍴 At stations
🚉 Kawaguchiko (Odakyu Line from Shinjuku Station; change at Otsuki)
♿ Few ❓ Tours; buses also run from Shinjuku to Kawaguchiko

Mount Fuji and Lake Ashi

EXCURSIONS

Downtown Kyoto

INFORMATION

Distance 318 miles

Time 2 hours 37 minutes by bullet train (*shinkansen*)

✉ Tourist Information Center (TIC): Kyoto Tower, Higashi-Shiokojicho, Shimogyo-ku, Kyoto

☎ TIC: 075/371–5649

◷ Sites: vary. Typically: Mar–Oct: daily 9–5. Nov–Feb 9–4. TIC: Mon–Fri 9–5; Sat 9–12

🍴 Plenty at and near station, in city and near major shrines

🚉 Kyoto (from Tokyo Station)

♿ Few

💰 Moderate–Expensive

❓ Tours from Tokyo (day tour too rushed) and within Kyoto. Avoid weekends and peak vacation periods. Arrange accommodations in advance, or at TIC early in the day. Good free maps; city guide in English

KYOTO

Kyoto, 318 miles from Tokyo, was Japan's capital for more than 1,000 years, the home of the emperor even while power resided elsewhere. It became the chief center of art and religion, and remained the cultural center even after it ceased to be the capital in 1868. It was spared the bombing that devastated most Japanese cities in 1945.

Don't be put off by first impressions. Although the area around the station looks like any modern Japanese city, narrow old streets and traditional shops are just a short walk away. Kyoto National Museum has fine archeological and art collections. The Imperial Palace in the center of the city, built in 1855, lost its role soon after the emperor moved to Tokyo. Of more interest is Nijo Castle, built in 1603 by the *shogun* Ieyasu Tokugawa (► 8), to mark his seizure of power. Most temples and shrines, although on the city's outskirts, are easily accessible. These are a few highlights.

Kiyomizu-dera Beautifully positioned on a hillside, this temple ("Clear Water") has a famous wide veranda giving a view over the city. Its pagoda, painted bright vermilion on the underside, is a landmark.

Chion-in The chief temple of the Buddhist Jodo sect is enormous, and brilliantly painted and decorated. The main buildings date from the 17th century. The belfry houses the biggest bell in Japan, cast in 1633; it takes 17 men to ring it.

Heian Shrine The massive red *torii* gateway (made of steel) and shrine buildings were built in 1895 to mark the 1,100th anniversary of

Kyoto's founding but their style echoes that of the first imperial palace. The gardens are famous for their spring blossoms and colors of fall.

The huge torii *at the entrance to Heian Shrine*

Ginkakuji (Silver Pavilion) This was built as a villa for a retired 15th-century *shogun*, Yoshimasa Ashikaga, whose intention to cover it with silver was never carried out, although the name stuck. In the other original building, the Togudo, Yoshimasa devised the tea ceremony that is performed to this day. The gardens are renowned for their ascetic formality and balance.

Kinkakuji (Golden Pavilion) Built in 1397 as a country retreat for a *shogun*, this three-story jewel covered in gold leaf became a temple after his death. What you see now is a replica: the original was destroyed in a fire started by a disturbed priest in 1950.

Ryoanji Temple Zen Garden Japanese garden lovers argue endlessly over the merits of raked gravel and carefully positioned rocks, the features of this austere garden. Most foreigners are politely mystified.

Kyoto transportation

The city is bigger than it looks.

- **Walking** from one shrine or garden to others nearby is delightful, but a route linking the important sights would be 12 miles long.
- **Bicycles** are a good way to get around: ask at the TIC.
- **Subways** runs north–south and east–west, but it's more convenient to take a bus.
- **Railroads** connect some sights.
- **Public transportation buses** cover all areas.
  The TIC has a route map.
- **Tour buses** are expensive and visit only a few sights.

WHAT'S ON

January	*Dezomeshiki* (Jan 6): Acrobatic displays by firemen on the top of tall bamboo ladders on Chuo-dori, Harumi.
	Young Adults' Day: Tens of thousands of 20-year-olds troop to the Meiji Shrine (▶ 30), the young women dressed in their finest kimonos.
February	*Setsubun Bean-Throwing Festival* (Feb 3): Held at many shrines and temples to drive away evil and invite good fortune.
March	*Doll festival*: Displays of dolls.
	Golden Days holiday: Millions of people travel to their family homes or on vacation.
mid May	*Sanja Matsuri*: Three-day festival and parades of portable shrines at Asakusa Kannon (Sensoji) Temple (▶ 49).
June	*Sanno Matsuri Festival* (Jun 10–16): At Hie Jinja, parades and processions carry portable shrines through Akasaka.
July	*Sumida River Fireworks*: First held in 1773, this is Japan's biggest firework display, with 20,000 fireworks and one million people attending.
August	*O-Bon*: Buddhist temple festivals honor the dead. Dancing, fireworks, and floating lanterns (each representing a soul) are floated on open water at night.
	Fukagawa Festival of Tomioka Hachimangu Shrine: See one hundred portable shrines.
October	*Oeshiki Festival* (Oct 11–13): Night lantern procession at Hommonji Buddhist Temple.
November	*Emperor Meiji's birthday festival* (Nov 3): At Meiji Shrine.
	Shichi-go-san (Nov 15): Three-, five-, and seven-year old children—many of them dressed in traditional kimonos—are taken to shrines.
December	*Gishi-sai* (evening of Dec 14): Honors the 47 *ronin* at Sengakuji Temple (▶ 33).
	Hagoita-ichi (Dec 17–19): Sensoji Temple, Asakusa (▶ 49). Traditional battledore fair and market. *Hagoita* are paddle-shaped bats used to hit the shuttlecock in the traditional game of *hanetsuki*.
	Emperor's Birthday (Dec 23): The Imperial Palace grounds are open.
	New Year holiday (Dec 28–Jan 3): Businesses close down, along with many attractions.

TOKYO's
top 25 sights

The sights are shown on the inside front cover and inside back cover,
numbered **1–25** from west to east across the city

METROPOLITAN GOVERNMENT OFFICES

HIGHLIGHTS

- The 45th-floor observatories, 663 feet high
- Surreal skyscrapers of Shinjuku
- Views of parks and distant downtown area
- Glimpse of Mount Fuji (1 day in 5)
- Sunset and night views
- Multiscreen video history
- Sculptures of human figures in plaza
- Exterior granite—white from Spain, dark from Sweden

INFORMATION

- ✚ C4
- ✉ Tokyo Metropolitan Government Offices, 2-8-1 Nishi-Shinjuku, Shinjuku-ku
- ☎ 5388—2267
- 🕐 Tue–Fri 9:30–5:30; Sat, Sun, and national holidays 9:30–7:30. Closed Tue if Mon a national holiday, and Dec 29–Jan 3
- 🍴 Snack bar on 45th floor; countless restaurants in nearby buildings
- Ⓢ Shinjuku
- 🚇 Shinjuku
- ♿ Very good
- 💰 Free
- ↔ Shinjuku Station (► 27), Japanese Sword Museum (► 29)

Above: the twin towers of the Metropolitan Government Offices

These striking, grandiose towers and their plazas were planned in the booming 1980s, and opened in 1991. On a clear day, the view from the top is unrivaled, with impressive silver and black towers rising all around.

Vantage point Each of the twin towers of Building No. 1 has an observatory on the 45th floor. It makes no difference which tower you choose: the elevators whisk you to the top in less than a minute. On a clear day the view is the most spectacular in Tokyo, with futuristic skyscrapers in the foreground, the green islands of the Meiji Shrine Inner Garden and Shinjuku Garden beyond, and the Imperial Palace, Ginza, and Tokyo Bay to the east. If you are lucky, you'll see Mount Fuji's perfect cone far away on the southwestern horizon.

Growth area In the days of the shogunate, Shinjuku was still a day's march from the capital, Edo (now Tokyo). Weary travelers coming from the west would stop at its inns to bathe and rest, dine, and visit one of the many houses of pleasure. With the coming of the railways, Shinjuku became a major junction. As late as 1970, Shinjuku was known mainly for its station, red-light district and sewage treatment works. When investors looked for alternatives to central Tokyo, Shinjuku had an important advantage: it seemed to survive earthquakes better than other areas. The first highrise was the Keio Plaza Hotel, put up by one of the railroad-department store combines. The Mitsui and Sumitomo office buildings soon followed. Then the city government decided to move to Shinjuku and commissioned Kenzo Tange to design a new complex to house the offices, on a scale to match its 6-trillion-yen annual budget.

2

SHINJUKU STATION

Twice a day, a tidal wave of humanity pours through Japan's busiest station—three to four million commuters, shoppers, and schoolchildren stream along its underground passages, heading for a dozen exits, and changing trains.

Human anthill Subway lines and JR railway lines meet at Shinjuku; private lines feed customers to their own department stores right above the station. The famous people-pushers operate at rush hour (*rashawa* in Japanese), packing as many bodies as they can into each carriage, giving them a final shove to let the doors close and then bowing as the train pulls out. It's worth experiencing—once—but not as an introduction to the system. Learn your way around at a quieter time first.

Exits You can walk more than a half a mile underground (more if you get lost). One long concourse on the west side links the station complex to many of Shinjuku's skyscrapers, including the Metropolitan Government Offices. Here and there, the homeless, who have somehow dropped through the cracks of Japan's tightly knit society, find a place to sleep, cocooned in cardboard cartons. To the hurrying crowds they seem invisible. The east exit leads to the My City building with several stories of good eating places and into a maze of alleys and the varied night entertainment of Kabukicho.

HIGHLIGHTS

- Organized chaos of rush hour
- People-pushers
- My City restaurant complex
- Department stores above station
- Underground city
- Harangues by fringe groups of far right and left
- Camera stores near station
- Takashimaya Times Square development on south side of station
- Kabukicho nightlife

INFORMATION

- ✚ D4
- ✉ Shinjuku-ku
- 🕐 4:30AM–1AM
- 🍴 Innumerable eating places of every kind
- Ⓢ Shinjuku
- 🚉 Shinjuku
- ♿ Few
- 💰 Free
- ↔ Metropolitan Government Offices (➤ 26), Kabukicho (➤ 80)

Clear directions help you find your way around Shinjuku Station

3

SHINJUKU NATIONAL GARDEN

INFORMATION

- ✚ E5
- ✉ 11 Naitocho, Shinjuku-ku
- ☎ 3350–0151
- 🕐 Tue–Sun 9–4:30. Closed Mon except at cherry-blossom time
- 🍴 Snacks
- 🚇 Shinjuku Gyoen-mae. Take the south exit and turn right
- 🚉 Shinjuku
- ♿ Few
- 💰 Moderate
- ↔ Shinjuku Station (➤ 27)

Expansive and verdant, the 150-acre Shinjuku National Garden is the perfect place for a stroll especially in April when thousands come to walk and picnic under some 1,900 of their beloved flowering cherry trees.

Origins The Shinjuku garden is one of the surpisingly large green spaces that relieve the concrete monotony of the city. It was once the estate of the powerful leader (*daimyo*) of the Naito clan—one of the Tokugawa shoguns who parceled out the land around their Edo stronghold to lesser lords whose duty was to defend the approaches. Following the over-throw of the shogunate and restoration of imperial power in 1868, it came into the hands of the emperor. After World War II, it was opened to the public as a national park.

Garden sights Landscaped with little hills, ponds, and bridges, the park includes greenhouses filled with tropical plants, an English country garden, a French formal garden, and a Japanese garden with a Chinese-style pavilion.

Each year, at cherry-blossom time, large crowds—guided by the daily blossom reports on TV—are drawn to see almost 2,000 trees, their white or pink petals blowing like snow in the wind. The biggest, most per-fect blooms of Japan's national flower, the chrysanthemum, are on show September to November.

The English garden in Shinjuku National Garden

JAPANESE SWORD MUSEUM

Gleaming and flawless, the blades kept at this museum are up to 900 years old, deadly weapons transmuted by age and beauty into works of art. You can see why they were credited with magical power.

The museum This box-shaped building on stilts, hidden in a residential street southwest of the Shinjuku skyscrapers, holds some of Japan's most revered cultural treasures.

The art The atmosphere is almost religious, the handful of visitors gazing in awe at swords that probably sliced off *samurai* heads. The armor on display highlights the defensive measures taken to try to ward off the flashing blades, including plenty of padding around the neck. Amazingly detailed leaflets in English explain the complex terminology associated with these weapons and their manufacture. Repeated folding and hammering produces a layered, resilient steel blade. This is coated in clay, except for the edge, heated in a furnace, and plunged into cold water. Thus tempered, the edge becomes diamond hard, able to cut through bone and inferior metal. Some swordmasters from as early as the 12th and 13th centuries signed their work, but others can be identified from the wavy tempering patterns along the blades. Several of the blades on display have been declared National Treasures, quite literally beyond price as nothing like them would ever come onto the market.

Getting there If you enjoy walking, visit the Sword Museum on the way between Shinjuku and the northwestern gate of the Meiji Shrine garden. You may need to ask the way. If you don't speak any Japanese, just say *Bijutsu Token*, or draw a picture of a curved blade and show it to a policeman or anybody who looks helpful.

HIGHLIGHTS

- 12th-century Heian period *tachi* sword
- 13th- to 14th-century Kamakura-period swords
- 17th-century Edo-period decorative swords
- Full *samurai* armor
- Decorated stirrups
- Swordmaking display
- Explanation of hardening and tempering
- Scabbard collection
- Excellent literature in English

INFORMATION

- C5
- 4-25-10 Yoyogi, Shibuya-ku
- 3379-1386
- Tue–Sun 9–4. Closed Dec 28–Jan 4
- Sangubashi
- Good
- Moderate
- Metropolitan Government Offices (▶ 26), Shinjuku Station (▶ 27), Meiji Shrine (▶ 30)

A samurai helmet

29

5

MEIJI SHRINE

HIGHLIGHTS

- 175 acres of wooded park
- Giant *torii* (gates)
- Shrine hall of cypress wood
- Folded paper prayers on bushes
- Cherry blossoms in spring
- Iris garden in summer
- Winter ice carvings
- Treasure Museum
- Wedding processions

INFORMATION

- ✚ D6
- ✉ 1-1 Yoyogi, Shibuya-ku
- ☎ 3379–5111
- ◷ Sunrise–sunset. Closed third Fri of each month
- ⊙ Meijijingu-mae
- ⊟ Harajuku, Sangubashi
- ♿ Few
- ⛶ Free
- ⟷ Japanese Sword Museum (➤ 29), Harajuku (➤ 31), Yoyogi Park (➤ 31), Ota Museum (➤ 53)

The Meiji Shrine

It's a pleasure to walk through the woods to the national focal point of the Shinto religion. Here, people mark important stages of their lives. Babies are brought for their first temple visit and newlyweds come to have marriages blessed.

The shrine The reign of Emperor Meiji (1868–1912) saw Japan transformed from a medieval to a modern state. The shrine was built in 1920 to honor him and his empress: in accordance with the beliefs of the day they had been declared divine. The shrine was destroyed by fire in 1945 air raids, but rebuilt in the original classical design. The great *torii* (gates) are made from 1,700-year-old cypress trees from Taiwan. The 150-acre inner gardens are noted for more than 100,000 trees, sent from all over Japan when the gardens were created in 1920. The Treasure Museum at the northern end of the gardens houses royal clothes and possessions.

Occasions Babies dressed in their best are usually brought by proud parents on Thursdays, and you can often see wedding processions—some in traditional costume and some in Western dress. The main festival is on November 3, Emperor Meiji's birthday.

HARAJUKU

The street scene in this neighborhood is a bizarre parade of the young and would-be young in black leather and tiny miniskirts even on arctic days. Hair is greased in 1950s styles, bleached blond, or dyed green—and that's on the boys.

East of the station Across the street from Harajuku Station, Takeshita-dori is a magnet for teenagers, an alley lined by stalls selling colored glasses, music tapes, fast food, coffee, and clothing at prices that are bargains, at least by Tokyo standards. Running parallel is the tree-lined Omotesando-dori, the street that Tokyoites think of as their Champs Elysées, lined with elegant, expensive boutiques. The Ota Museum (► 53), just off it, houses a superb collection of *ukiyo-e* (woodblock prints; ► 53, panel). One of the city's best antiques and flea markets is held on the first and fourth Sundays of each month, is just to the north, off Meiji-dori, near the Togo Shrine (► 57). The shrine itself honors Admiral Togo who was the architect of the Japanese navy that defeated the Russian fleet in 1905.

Yoyogi Park The green space west of the station and next to the gounds of Meiji Shrine was a Japanese army camp during World War II, and afterwards the base of U.S. occupying forces. It was also the site of the 1964 Olympic Games village and retains the sports arenas built there. A few years ago, the noisy rock bands and street dancers that on Sundays used to fill Inogashira-dori, south of the park, were banned. Across the now-quiet road is the National Yoyogi Sports Center and Stadium, designed for the Olympics by Kenzo Tange. The structure's swooping, steel-suspension roof evokes the appearance of those on traditional Japanese temples.

HIGHLIGHTS

- Takeshita-dori street market
- Omotesando-dori shops
- Ota Museum's woodblock prints
- Togo Shrine
- Bi-monthly flea markets (► 75)
- Yoyogi Park, gardens
- Sports center
- NHK Broadcasting Center tours (► 62)
- Teen fashion scene

INFORMATION

- D6; E7
- Harajuku, Shibuya-ku
- 24 hours
- A very wide choice
- Meijijingu-mae
- Harajuku
- Few
- Free
- Meiji Shrine (► 30), Ota Museum (► 53)

Above: the Togo Shrine, off Meiji-dori

31

7

YEBISU GARDEN PLACE

HIGHLIGHTS

- Museum of Photography
- Mitsukoshi department store
- Beer museum
- HDTV and virtual reality demonstrations
- "Top of Yebisu" views
- Westin Tokyo Hotel
- 1930s-style German beer hall

INFORMATION

- ✛ F10
- ✉ 1 Mita, Meguro-ku and 4 Ebisu, Shibuya-ku
- ☎ General information: 5423–7111
- ◷ Tue–Wed, Sat–Sun 10–6; Thu–Fri 10–8. Museums: closed Mon
- 🍴 Beer hall; restaurants; fast-food outlets
- Ⓔ Ebisu
- Ⓔ Ebisu
- ♿ Good
- Free (except Museum of Photography)
- ❓ Chain of moving walkways from JR Ebisu Station. Maps and signs say Ebisu for the area and station, Yebisu for the development

The old Sapporo Brewery site is one of Tokyo's most imaginative developments, with its two brilliantly designed museums, a vast Bavarian beer hall, luxury hotel, and from atop Yebisu Garden Palace Tower, its sweeping city views.

The beer connection As a serious polluter, the red-brick brewery had to go, but the company held on to the site, moved its offices here, and created 1,000 luxury apartments. Some of the brewing equipment went into a beer museum, where it takes on the quality of sculpture. The brewing process is explained and in a virtual reality brewery tour you see what it's like to be a molecule going through fermentation. Then you get to sample a glass of the product (▶ 61).

Museum of Photography The second museum on the site, the Tokyo Metropolitan Museum of Photography (▶ 54) showcases the latest photographic techniques and displays of historic equipment. Don't miss the History of Images display in the basement. There is an interesting permanent collection of early photographs.

Time out Along with the Mitsukoshi department store, there's a big restaurant complex with a huge beer hall reminiscent of a Munich *bierkeller* of the 1930s. The Westin Tokyo Hotel is worth a visit; there's a good view from the bar or restaurant on the 23rd floor.

Above: Museum of Photography
Right: A mash copper in the Beer Museum

8

SENGAKUJI TEMPLE

This temple offers an insight into Japanese values: the heroes commemorated are still honored for their loyalty, single-mindedness, efficiency, ruthlessness, and collective action. They lived and died by the samurai *code.*

Code of honor Sengakuji was one of the three great temples of Edo, and it is still one of the most important in Tokyo. After their lord Naganori Asano was unjustly forced into suicide in 1701, Yoshitaka Oishi and 47 loyal retainers (*ronin*, meaning "masterless *samurai*") vowed to avenge him. They raided the castle of the chief instigator, Yoshinaka Kira, beheaded him, and carried the head in triumph to Asano's tomb at Sengakuji. They in turn were required by their code to commit ritual suicide, a duty they accepted as an honor. Before killing himself, Oishi chivalrously returned Kira's head to his family. The receipt for "one head" signed by the temple priests who took charge of it can still be seen in the museum. The story spread quickly and has captured Japanese imaginations ever since. It has been told and retold as *kabuki* (▶ 78) and puppet theater, in movies, and on television.

The tombs and museum Oishi and his followers were all buried at Sengakuji. The 47 simple stones are arranged in a square, with the larger tombs of Asano and his wife, and Oishi and his son, nearby. Clouds of smoke rise from incense sticks placed in front of each tomb by the many worshippers who come to honor the dead heroes. In the museum, there are polychrome statues believed to be exact likenesses of the 47 so detailed that you can study every aspect of their dress. Their armor and weapons, including some fearsome spiked maces, are displayed separately.

HIGHLIGHTS

- Sanmon, the main gate
- Shoro, the Bell Tower
- Tombs of the 47 *ronin*
- Tombs of Asano and Oishi
- Temple gardens
- Polychrome statues of the 47 *ronin*
- *Samurai* weapons and armor
- Original clothing

INFORMATION

- H10
- 2-11-1 Takanawa, Minato-ku
- 3441–5560
- Daily 9–4
- Small restaurants in nearby street
- Sengakuji (exit A2 and head uphill)
- Few
- Temple: free. Museum: inexpensive

Above: tombstones at Sengakuji Temple

33

9

TOKYO TOWER

HIGHLIGHTS

- Observation decks at 492 feet and 820 feet
- General view from 820 feet
- View of Mount Fuji—(1 day in 5)
- Tokyo Tower Trick Art Gallery
- Aquarium
- Towerland electric arcade

INFORMATION

- ✚ H8
- ✉ 4-2-8 Shiba Koen (Park), Minato-ku
- ☎ 3433–5111
- ◐ Mar 16–Nov 15: daily 9–8 (Aug 9–9). Nov 16–Mar 15: daily 9–7
- 🍴 Snack bars and cafés
- 🚇 Kamiyacho, Onarimon
- ♿ Few (possible to first level)
- 💲 Expensive
- ↔ Zojoji Temple (➤ 35)

Tokyo's answer to the Eiffel Tower outdoes the original in height by a margin of about 30 feet. Come on a clear day for a fine view of the Sumida River and Tokyo Bay, Ginza, and the Imperial Palace.

The tower At Kamiyacho subway station, emerge from Exit 1 and head uphill. It takes about seven minutes to walk to the foot of the tower. Built in 1958 to carry television transmissions, it now broadcasts all Tokyo's channels as well as FM radio stations. Cameras at the 820-foot level keep an eye on the city's notorious traffic and send pictures to a central control room, which is the source of the information flashed up along the expressways. The tower is the world's tallest freestanding iron structure. The view from the 492-foot level is not remarkable; you need to pay extra to go to 820 feet where the view is worthwhile if the day is clear enough.

The extras There is is a mixed bag of attractions around the base and lower levels, all expensive. An aquarium, on the second floor, holds 50,000 fish of some 800 varieties, and its shop sells many colorful species. On the fifth floor is the Trick Art Gallery where 3D pictures are painted in special paints to create unusual effects. TEPCO, the electric company, runs a play area with video games and a 3D movie theater.

Top: the view from the 1,092-foot-high Tokyo Tower
Above: Tokyo Tower by night

ZOJOJI TEMPLE

Among the city's touching sights are the rows of little statues of Jizobosatsu, the protector of the souls of stillborn children. Some are dressed in baby clothes; all hold whirling toy windmills.

The temple Zojoji, the chief temple of the Jodo-Buddhist sect, was founded in 1393. It was the family temple of the Tokugawa clan, and when Ieyasu Tokugawa became *shogun* with Edo as his power base, he set about enlarging and beautifying it. The *Sanmon*, (two-storied) main gate, built in 1605 in Chinese Tang Dynasty style, is a rare example of early Edo-period architecture in Tokyo. All the other buildings at Zojoji were destroyed in 1945 and were later replaced by concrete replicas. An ancient black image of Amita Buddha is carried in procession three times a year, on January 15, May 15, and September 15.

The gardens Near the Sanmon, a cedar tree planted by President Ulysses S. Grant in 1879 also miraculously survived the 1945 air raids and fires. As at many temples, prayers written on folded paper are tied like white flowers to the smaller trees and bushes. Nearby, the outlines of two feet said to be those of Buddha are incised in a rock that was probably brought from China (like similar work in the Tokyo National Museum). Also in the garden is a large temple bell, said to have been cast in 1673 from the ornamental hairpins of court ladies. Colorful and sad at the same time are the multiple images of Jizobosatsu, or Jizo, the Buddhist equivalent of an angel, dressed in red baby bonnets. Mothers who have experienced stillbirth or who have had an abortion, may dedicate an image of the deity and decorate it with baby clothes, toys, and little windmills.

HIGHLIGHTS

- Sanmon, the restored 1605 gate
- Main hall of the temple
- Great Bell of 1673, 10 feet high
- Cedar tree planted by President Grant
- Stone engraving of Buddha's feet
- Gardens, flowering trees in spring
- Folded paper prayers on bushes
- Multiple images of Jizo

INFORMATION

- ✚ J8
- ✉ Shiba Koen, Minato-ku. (Lies across the street below Tokyo Tower)
- 🕐 Sunrise–sunset
- 🚇 Onarimon, Shiba-koen
- ♿ Few
- 💲 Free
- ↔ Tokyo Tower (➤ 34)

Above: little statues of Jizo are dressed in red baby bonnets

35

11

IMPERIAL PALACE EAST GARDEN

INFORMATION

- ➕ J5
- ✉ Chiyoda-ku
- 🕐 Tue–Thu, Sat, Sun 9–4 (no entry after 3PM). Closed Dec 25–Jan 5
- 🚇 Otemachi, Takebashi
- 🚉 Tokyo
- ♿ Few
- 💰 Free
- ↔ National Museum of Modern Art (➤ 37)
- ❓ More of Imperial Palace grounds can be seen by special permission. For information ☎ 3213–1111 ext 485. Tickets must be collected day before visit. Passports required. Tour times: 10–11:30AM, 1:30–4PM

This was once part of the emperor's private garden. Bordered by the massive palace walls, the carefully tended gardens and their water features offer a haven for city workers from the nearby financial district.

Gateway The Imperial Palace East Garden (Kokyo Higashi Gyoen) is a vast green space in the heart of the city. It was once the biggest fortress in the world, the *shogun*'s castle of Edo, which after 1868 became the site of the Imperial Palace. The East Garden is only a fraction of the whole, but is still big enough for a long walk. The usual entrance is through the Otemon, near the Palace Hotel; it was the main castle gate, one of 36 in the outer walls, elaborately designed for defense. If you think you hear the ghosts of warring *samurai* shouting, it's probably the police martial arts class in the hall next to the guard house. A small museum near the gate shows exhibits from the imperial collections.

The sights A short walk brings you to the massive foundations of the castle keep, crowning a low hill. Notice the perfect fit of the huge stones in the walls: mortar free, they were designed to withstand earthquakes. There's a good view over the gardens and the city from the top, but imagine—there was once a tower here standing five stories high, and the whole hill was densely packed with buildings. The tower was destroyed by fire in 1657, and most of the remaining buildings were razed after the Meiji emperor was restored to power in 1868. The gardens are beautifully tended, and there is always something in bloom, notably the azaleas and cherry blossoms in spring and the irises in summer. Huge carp somehow survive in the uninviting moats, and cormorants perch in wait for smaller fry.

12

NATIONAL MUSEUM OF MODERN ART

This is the place to see the best of 20th-century painting by Japanese artists, many of them influenced by the West. Here their creations are exhibited side by side with major works by their European contemporaries.

The museum The National Museum of Modern Art (Kokuritsu Kindai Bijutsukan) is in Kitanomaru Park, formerly a part of the Imperial Palace gardens. The severe concrete box of a building was designed by Yoshiro Taniguchi and built in 1969. Inside, the galleries are spacious and skillfully lit. The ground floor houses temporary exhibitions, the top three the permanent collection. Many foreign visitors are initially drawn to the familiar work of Klee and Chagall, and the fine portrait of Alma Mahler by Kokoschka; and then turn to works of Japanese painters who worked in France and Germany early in the 20th century. Tetsugoro Yorozu's nudes might almost be by Matisse, and Tsuguharu Fujita was practically an honorary Frenchman. Some of the most ravishing pictures are by those who developed the Japanese idiom in new ways—as in Kanzan Shimomura's luminous *Autumn Among Trees*, Gyokudo Kawai's 12-panel *Parting Spring*, and Shinsui Ito's *Snowy Evening*.

Crafts gallery Just across Kitanomaru Park is an impressive brick building of 1911—once headquarters of the Imperial Guard. It now houses exhibitions of 20th-century craft work, including fine textiles, graphic design, ceramics, lacquer-work, and metalwork, both traditional and modern.

HIGHLIGHTS

- *Ascension*, Tatsuoki Nambata
- *Portrait of Alma Mahler*, Kokoschka
- *Deep Woods*, Keigetsu Matsubayashi
- *Bathing*, Taketaro Shinkai
- *Stream*, bronze nude by Taimu Tatahata

INFORMATION

- ✛ J4
- ✉ 3 Kitanomaru Koen, Chiyoda-ku
- ☎ 3214–2561
- 🕐 Tue–Sun 10–5; Fri (in summer) 10–8. Closed Tue if Mon a national holiday
- Ⓣ Takebashi
- ♿ Good
- 💹 Moderate
- ↔ Imperial Palace East Garden (▶ 36)

Nude Beauty, *Tetsugoro Yorozu*

37

13

YASUKUNI SHRINE

Japan's war dead are remembered at this most important of Shinto shrines. The adjacent War Memorial Museum, Yushukan, honors those killed in action and includes a suicide plane, military memorabilia, and weaponry.

HIGHLIGHTS

- Steel *torii* weighing 100 tons
- Flocks of white doves
- Japanese garden and flowering trees
- *Samurai* armor and weapons
- Carrier-borne aircraft "Judy"
- Man-guided torpedo
- Oka, rocket plane replica
- Tributes to fallen heroes
- Historic newsreels
- Recording of the emperor's 1945 surrender speech

INFORMATION

- ✚ H4
- ✉ 3-1-1 Kudankita, Chiyoda-ku
- ☎ Museum: 3261–8326
- 🕐 Shrine: daily sunrise–sunset. Museum: Oct–Feb: daily 9–4:30. Mar–Sep: daily 9–5. Closed Jun 22–23, Dec 28–31
- 🍴 Drinks stand
- 🚇 Kudanshita (Exit 1)
- ♿ Good
- 🎫 Shrine: free. Museum: inexpensive

Spirits and sacrifices Yasukuni shrine on Kudan Hill, northwest of the Imperial Palace, was founded on the orders of Emperor Meiji in 1869 for the worship of the spirits, the *mitima*, of those who had sacrificed their lives in the battles for the restoration the previous year. Now it honors the 2.5 million who died "in the defense of the empire" in the years that followed, although it is controversial because these deaths mainly occurred in aggressive wars in China, the Pacific, and Southeast Asia. Flocks of white doves live on the grounds of the shrine.

Instruments of destruction The museum commemorates the Russo-Japanese War of 1905, the invasion of Manchuria, and World War II. Exhibits range from *samurai* armor and swords to 20th-century guns, tanks, and planes,

including a carrier-borne bomber and a replica Oka, a *kamikaze* rocket-powered winged bomb. Newsreels of the last days of World War II show fleets of B-29s showering bombs on Japan, *kamikaze* pilots taking off on their one-way missions, the devastation caused by the atomic bombs, and the emperor's surrender speech in August 1945.

Statue of Masujiro Ohomura near the entrance to Yasukuni Shrine

14

NATIONAL DIET BUILDING

This Japanese Art-Deco building capped by a stepped pyramid, which houses Japan's national legislature, is opulent inside. Sessions—which you can watch from the public gallery or on closed circuit TV—can be lively or tedious.

The building A competition was held in 1918 for designs for a new Imperial Diet Building (Kokkaigijido); work started in 1920 and took 16 years to finish. Japanese militarism was growing at the time, and the last thing the generals who controlled the government wanted was a genuine parliament. The constant interference sparked the withdrawal of Julia Morgan, the architect, who designed William Randolph Hearst's San Simeon castle and other structures in the United States. When the odd-looking building finally opened, the Imperial Diet had become no more than a rubber stamp. Not until 1946 was there the first general election with universal suffrage, with women voting for the first time. The following year the new National Diet met, replacing the old Imperial Diet.

Visits When the Diet is in session, you can sit in the public gallery of either house. You need your passports and, for some sessions, a letter of introduction from your embassy. Admission is by token, which you can get at the office on the north side of the building. Riots in the Diet are not unknown, but proceedings are rarely so exciting—as you can see on the TV screen in the entrance hall. Most speakers read from prepared scripts which address contentious issues only in the vaguest of terms. When the Diet is not in session, organized tours take you into the 491-member House of Representatives, the 252-member House of Councillors (Japan's senate), and a selection of other rooms.

HIGHLIGHTS

- Marble halls and bronze doors
- House of Councillors
- Imperial throne
- House of Representatives
- Public gallery
- Stained-glass ceilings
- Emperor's Room
- Lacquer and mother-of-pearl decoration
- Avenue of gingko trees, golden in the fall

INFORMATION

- ✚ H6
- ✉ Chiyoda-ku
- ☎ Upper house: 3581–5111. Lower house: 3581–3111
- 🕐 Tue–Sun 10–4:30. Closed national holidays, and Dec 27–Jan 3
- 🍴 Snack bar
- 🚇 Kokkaigijido-mae, Nagatacho
- ♿ Good
- 🎫 Free
- ⬆ Hie Jinja shrine (▶ 56)
- ❓ Guided tours of the building when the Diet is not in session. Carry your passport

15

HIBIYA PARK

HIGHLIGHTS

- Bonsai shops
- Ponds and fountains
- Floral borders, even in winter
- Outdoor auditorium concerts
- Imperial Hotel, opposite
- Intricate supports for precious trees
- Hibiya City—winter skating

INFORMATION

- ✚ J6
- ✉ Chiyoda-ku
- ☎ 3501–6428
- ⏰ Dawn–11PM
- 🍴 Good restaurant; snack bars
- Ⓢ Hibiya, Uchisaiwaicho
- Ⓡ Yurakucho
- ♿ Good
- 💰 Free
- ↔ Ginza (▶ 41), Idemitsu Museum of Arts (▶ 52)

Chrysanthemums are highly prized in Japan

In this tranquil corner of Tokyo, the city's first public park, lovers find private retreats, secretaries from nearby offices eat their box lunches, and tired tourists rest up from sightseeing.

Six acres Hibiya park is a green extension of the Imperial Palace Outer Garden. On one side of Hibiya park are the ministry buildings of Kasumigaseki, the edge of Ginza is only a block away on the other. In the park itself fountains play, waterbirds swim on the ponds, and gardeners groom the flowerbeds and trim the trees into impeccable order. The constructions of rope and wood they build to support precious specimens through the winter snows are works of art. There are public tennis courts and restaurants, a shop sells perfect little bonsai trees, and on weekend afternoons occasional pop and rock concerts take place in the outdoor auditorium. Mostly though, people come to stroll and sit, away from crowds and traffic. Visitors from out of town always seem to want to be photographed here.

The vicinity Facing the southeast side of the park is the massive Imperial Hotel (1970), which replaced Frank Lloyd Wright's 1920s original, deemed too small and too difficult to maintain and torn down in 1967. The new hotel's vast lobby is one of Tokyo's favorite meeting points. Nearby Hibiya City, an office building and shopping complex, is modeled after New York's Rockefeller Plaza, with an outdoor skating-rink in winter. Across the Harumi-dori from the Imperial Hotel is the Dai-Ichi building—once General MacArthur's headquarters.

GINZA

The Ginza neighborhood may have the most expensive real estate on earth, and its stores and clubs have prices to match. On a par with New York's Fifth Avenue you can browse its elegant stores and stroll among Toyko's wealthiest citizens.

Shops The name Ginza derives from the silver mint that the *shogun* built in the area in 1612. Money attracts money, and merchants soon set up shops nearby. Their successors are the famous department stores of today, two of which—Wako and Mitsukoshi—stand at the heart of Ginza, the "Yon-chome" (4-chome). This is where the intersection of two main streets meet, Harumi-dori and Chuo-dori. On Sunday afternoons the latter is closed to vehicles; when the weather is fine, cafés put out tables and umbrellas. Prices are high in most stores. But not all the shopping is on a grand scale. Down the side streets, you can find boutiques and little specialty stores where prices are almost reasonable, along with hostess clubs and bars where they are outrageous. Restaurants can be extraordinarily expensive too, but you can find something sensibly priced at one of the department stores (▶ 73, panel).

Sights Ginza's wide, straight streets date from 1872, when a fire destroyed much of the area, which covers dozens of blocks. Although many buildings today are steel-and-glass and have neon signs, several late 19th-century buildings survive, including the Wako store with a famous clock tower, which is a landmark. Down Harumi-dori near Higashi-Ginza subway station is the rebuilt Kabuki-za Theater with matinée and evening performances on most days. Continue in the same direction and you will reach Tsukiji Fish Market and the Sumida River.

HIGHLIGHTS

- Ginza 4-chome crossing
- Lights of Ginza by night
- Wako's elegant displays
- Shoppers in designer clothing
- Basement food departments
- Mikimoto pearl shop
- Kabuki-za Theater
- Beer halls
- Side street discount shops
- Sunday strolling on Chuo-dori

INFORMATION

- K6–K7
- Chuo-ku
- 24 hours
- Countless restaurants and fast-food outlets
- Ginza, Higashi-Ginza
- Yurakucho
- Few
- Free
- Hibiya Park (▶ 40), Sony Center (▶ 42), Tsukiji Fish Market (▶ 44), Idemitsu Museum of Arts (▶ 52), Kabuki-za Theater (▶ 78)

17

SONY CENTER

HIGHLIGHTS

- Super-realistic video games
- Big screen HDTV
- Make your own video
- Tiny walkmans and VCRs
- Minidiscs
- Digital cameras
- Global positioning
- Playstation
- Super Audio CDs
- Transparent-cased equipment

INFORMATION

- ✚ K6
- ✉ 5-3-1 Ginza, Chuo-ku
- ☎ 3573–2371
- ◷ 11–7
- 🍴 Cafés on several levels; restaurants in same building
- Ⓖ Ginza
- Ⓡ Yurakucho
- ♿ Few
- 💲 Free
- ↔ Ginza (➤ 41)

The Sony Plaza

Here six floors of electronic marvels, including some devices that will not have yet reached your home town, are set up for hands-on testing. There's always a line of eager people waiting to test the latest Playstation.

Showroom Japan leads the world in consumer electronics, launching an endless succession of innovations. Sony—one of the biggest companies and the one that put "walkman" into the world's dictionaries—is in the forefront, and this center in Ginza is its shop window. Here you can not only see new products but also try them out. If you haven't yet caught up with Super Audio CDs, Entertainment Robots, or digital cameras, this is your chance. Miniaturization is a specialty and you'll see tiny cellular phones, personal CD players, minicams, and video recorders. Positioning equipment using earth satellites was top secret not so many years ago; now there are simple hand-held models that will tell you accurately where on earth you are and mark the spot on a map.

Demonstrations Now that everyone has a television, the industry has to produce something better and the marketing wizards have to persuade people to buy it. High definition television (HDTV) is already here; you can see its brilliantly crisp pictures on a huge screen. Check out the Air Board, a cordless, hand-held flat screen that uses wireless technology for portable viewing. Try the latest laptop computers with their built-in digital cameras and microphones that transmit your image and voice to other computers. Other tenants in the building include BMW, clothing stores, and many restaurants.

HAMA RIKU GARDEN

The scene at this tranquil 62-acre garden can have changed little since feudal lords came duck hunting here. Ponds, planted thickly with reeds and bamboo, provide cover for the hundreds of waterfowl.

The garden Now hemmed in between an expressway and the Sumida River, the Hama Rikyu Garden, also known as Hama Detached Palace Garden, was once part of the private game reserve of the Tokugawa *shogun*s and comprises water, woods, and gardens. It came into the hands of the imperial family in 1871 and was given to the city in 1945. Clever planting ensures that some species are always in bloom, and big areas are much more naturalistic and wild and less formal than in the typical Japanese garden. The river is tidal this close to its mouth, and seawater flows in and out of one of the ponds. Long causeway bridges with wisteria-covered trellises lead across the river to a replica of the picturesque Nakajima teahouse where Emperor Meiji entertained President Ulysses S. Grant and Mrs. Grant in 1879. The 300-year-old pine tree near the entrance was planted by one of the early *shogun*s.

River boats Apart from the pleasure of strolling in the garden, the best reason for a visit is to catch one of the frequent water buses for a cruise upriver to the traditional area of Asakusa, with its temple and small shops (► 16, 49). Boats leave the terminal at the eastern tip of the garden every half-hour or so, for the 45-minute trips, which gives you a completely different view of Tokyo. Nearby Hinoda Pier—a five-minute walk from Hamamatsucho station—is the terminus for other Tokyo Bay cruises including those to Shinagawa Aquarium (► 62), Palette Town (► 47), and bay sightseeing tours.

HIGHLIGHTS

- River views
- Duck lakes, once used for hunting
- Seawater tidal pond
- Causeway bridges
- Teahouse
- Japanese formal garden
- Peony garden
- Flowering trees, all year
- Precious trees wrapped up for winter
- River cruises

INFORMATION

- ✛ K8
- ✉ 1-1 Hamarikyuteien, Chuo-ku
- ☎ 3541–0200
- 🕐 Tue–Sun 9–4:30. Closed Dec 29–Jan 3
- 🚇 Shinbashi, Higashi-Ginza
- ♿ Few
- 🍴 Moderate
- ↔ Tsukiji Fish Market (► 44)

19

TSUKIJI FISH MARKET

HIGHLIGHTS

- Fish market, 5–7:30AM
- Buyers checking fish
- Auctioneers and their entourage
- Tuna auctions, 5:30–6:30AM
- Sunrise over Sumida River
- The wholesale market
- Restaurants
- Honganji Temple
- Pretty Namiyoke ("Wave Calm") Shrine
- Sushi breakfast

INFORMATION

➕ K7–L7–L8

✉ Tsukiji, Chuo-ku

🕐 Mon–Sat 5AM–3PM. Closed Sun, national holidays, and market holidays (check at tourist offices)

🍴 Superb sushi bars and many noodle stalls

🚇 Tsukiji, Higashi-Ginza

🎫 Free

↔ Ginza (➤ 41), Hama Rikyu Garden (➤ 43)

Set your alarm clock for 4:30AM and catch the first subway to Tsukiji Station. Tokyo's most amazing spectacle, the pre-dawn tuna auctions rewards you most thoroughly for getting out of bed at such an unearthly hour.

The auctions Since the Japanese are particular about their sushi and sashimi, seafood has to reach the consumer in perfect condition. An enormous industry ensures that it does, and 90 percent of the fish eaten in Tokyo passes through Tsukiji Fish Market in the Central Wholesale Market. The action begins at 5AM, when buyers inspect the giant bluefin tuna, smaller yellowfin, and aptly named "big eyes," flown in fresh from all over the world. At 5:30 the auctioneer rings a handbell and in seconds the first tuna are sold—some for a sum that would buy a small car.

The market In the neighboring wholesale market, 1,200 stalls sell every sort of fish and crustacean, most of them still jumping or crawling. Buyers for the city's restaurants and shops crowd the narrow alleys as struggling

masses of them are poured from one container to another, water floods onto the floor and into the shoes of the unwary (so wear boots or tie plastic bags over your footwear) and when you've seen enough, duck into one of the sushi bars (➤ 66) nearby for a Japanese breakfast.

A market trader prepares her stand in Tsukiji Fish Market

NATIONAL MUSEUM OF WESTERN ART

You may not have come to Tokyo to see masterpieces of European art, but the collection of this museum, mainly formed by one visionary in the early 20th century, is too good to miss.

The museum The National Museum of Western Art (Kokuritsu Seiyo Bijutsukan) is on the right of the main gate to Ueno Park from the JR station. The modernist concrete building, designed by Le Corbusier, holds the art collection of Kojiro Matsukata. Matsukata was a successful businessman who spent a lot of time in Europe in the early 20th century and developed a passion for the work of the French Impressionists. His collection eventually numbered hundreds of works, including some of the finest paintings by Monet, Renoir, Gauguin (in his pre-Tahiti period), and Van Gogh, over 50 of the most famous Rodin bronzes (including *The Thinker* and *The Burghers of Calais*, and El Greco's *The Crucifixion*. Matsukata kept them in Europe, but after World War II they were brought to Japan and bequeathed to the nation in his will. The museum was opened in 1959.

The growing collection Kojiro Matsukata's inspired acquisitions are still the museum's greatest strength, but the scope of a museum of Western art beyond one era and one country, and major purchases have filled the gaps. At one end of the time scale there are works by Old Masters, including Tintoretto, Rubens, and El Greco; moderns are represented by Max Ernst, Jackson Pollock, and others. You can stroll among the sculptures in the museum's courtyard; inside, good lighting does justice to the wonderful works of art. There are also some excellent traveling exhibitions.

HIGHLIGHTS

- *Crucifixion*, El Greco
- *Summer Evening Landscape in Italy*, Claude-Joseph Vernet
- *The Loving Cup*, D. G. Rossetti
- Rodin bronzes
- *Landscape of Brittany*, Gauguin
- *On the Boat*, Monet
- *Water Lilies*, Monet
- *Parisiennes in Algerian Costume*, Renoir
- *The Port of St. Tropez*, Signac
- *The Petrified Forest*, Ernst

INFORMATION

- L2
- Ueno Park, Taito-ku
- 3828–5131
- Tue–Sun 9:30–5. Closed Tue if Mon a national holiday, and Dec 26– Jan 3
- Drinks stand; snacks outside
- Ueno
- Ueno (Park exit)
- Good
- Expensive
- Tokyo National Museum (➤ 46), Shitamachi Museum (➤ 54), Ueno Zoo (➤ 62)

Above: Rodin's The Burghers of Calais *in the museum courtyard*

45

21

TOKYO NATIONAL MUSEUM

HIGHLIGHTS

- Jomon-era clay masks
- 3rd-century BC bronze bells
- Terra-cotta burial figures
- Decorative tiles
- Imari ware
- Noh costumes, 16th–18th centuries
- 1664 palanquin
- Sword collection
- Han Dynasty stone reliefs
- Tang Dynasty horses and camel

INFORMATION

- L1
- Ueno Park, Taito-ku
- 3822–1111
- Tue–Sun 9–4:30. Closed Tue if Mon a national holiday, and Dec 26–Jan 3
- A small restaurant serves snacks and light meals
- Ueno
- Ueno
- Good
- Moderate
- National Museum of Western Art (➤ 45), Shitamachi Museum (➤ 54), Ueno Zoo (➤ 62)

A great museum—and Tokyo National Museum is one—sparks your interest in fields you never thought about before. Here you can learn about every aspect of Japanese art and archeology and view a fine collection of other Asian art. The exhibits are simply breathtaking.

The Japanese collection The central Honkan building displays the finest of Japanese art: not only painting and sculpture, but calligraphy, ceramics including the celebrated Imari ware, kimons, swords, armor and *ukiyo-e* (woodblock prints; ➤ 53, panel). There are exquisite *noh* theater costumes, some dating from the 16th century. English explanations are limited mainly to names and dates.

Archeology The Heiseikan, the newest of the five main buildings of the Tokyo National Museum (Tokyo Kokuritsu Hakubutsukan), was built in 1999 and forms a new wing to the left of the Honkan building. It houses relics found in archaeological digs all over Japan: prehistoric flint axes, elaborate pottery from around 3000 BC, bronze bells, and sword blades. Many intriguing terra-cotta burial figures—musicians, horses, and wild boars—date from the 3rd to 6th centuries.

Other Asian art The Toyokan building includes exhibits of Chinese jade and bronzes, 1st-century stone reliefs, Tang Dynasty ceramic horses and a camel, precious porcelain, and textiles. Korea, Southeast Asia, Iran, Iraq, and even ancient Egypt are represented. Gondara Buddhist sculpture from Central Asia shows the influence of ancient Greek art during and after the time of Alexander the Great. Be sure to look inside the Hyokeikan building, built as a memorial for the marriage of the Meiji Crown Prince in 1909.

22

TOKYO BAY AREA

A vacant stretch of reclaimed land until not long ago, this latest mega development boasts an amazing collection of entertainment, shopping, and exhibition facilities, and even its own beach.

Palette Town Complex Start at Mega Web, a hands-on museum that showcases the latest in automotive technology. Included in the complex is Future World, a glimpse at future transportation with a 3D coaster ride, and a History Garage, that displays classic cars from the 1950s to the 1970s in nostalgic urban settings. Not far away, you can savor the bay views from the Giant Sky Wheel, the world's largest, or check out the NeoGeo World with its popular indoor roller coaster. The adjoining Sun Walk shopping complex includes restaurants and the women's mega mall, VenusFort, done in 18th-century style, sculptured fountains, and artificial "sky."

Decks, Joypolis, and Seaside Park Built to resemble a giant multi-storied passenger liner, the Decks shopping and entertainment complex has an array of boutiques and includes the Tokyo Joypolis, a virtual reality center with thrilling rides and many video games. The man-made beach at Seaside Park is popular for sunbathing in warm weather but as it is a harbor, the water here is not suitable for swimming.

Mediage, Aqua City, and Fuji Television At Mediage, along with movies you will find the mini funparks: Where the Wild Things Are, Airtight Garage, and the the Beatles' Yellow Submarine Adventure. The adjoining Aqua City retail complex has a Toys 'R' Us. Near the Daiba Station is the futuristic Fuji Television building with an observation deck, designed by architect Tange Kenzo, and opened in 1997.

HIGHLIGHTS

- Mega Web
- NeoGeo World
- Giant Sky Wheel
- History Garage
- VenusFort
- Decks Tokyo Beach
- Aqua City/Mediage
- Tokyo Joypolis
- View of Rainbow Bridge

INFORMATION

- ✚ Off map to south
- ✉ Rinkai-fukutoshin
- ☎ For information:
  Mega Web: 3599–0808
  VenusFort: 3599–0700
  (Women's shopping; men welcome)
  NeoGeo World: 3599–0800
  Giant Sky Wheel: 5500–2655
  Tokyo Joypolis: 5500–1801
  Aqua City 3599–4700
  Meidage: 5531 7800
- 🕐 Daily 10–10. Some hours vary
- 🍴 Restaurants and cafés
- Ⓨ Yurikamome line from Shimbashi Station to various stations
- 🚢 Hinode Pier to Odaiba Seaside Park
- ♿ Good to excellent
- 💲 Free to expensive
- ↔ Museum of Maritime Science (► 54)
- ❓ The area is reached via the impressive Rainbow Bridge by train or it is possible to walk at a charge of ¥300.

Above: the futuristic Fuji Television building   47

23

EDO-TOKYO MUSEUM

HIGHLIGHTS

- Audio-visual hall
- Hands-on exhibits
- Middle-Jomon period dwelling
- Nihonbashi Bridge
- Earthquake display
- Reconstructed Tokyo
- *Model A Ford*
- *Edo Castle*

INFORMATION

➕ N4

✉ 1-4-1 Yokoami, Sumida-ku

☎ 3626–9974

🕐 Daily 10–6 (Thu, Fri 8).
Closed Mon and Dec 28–Jan 4

🍴 Restaurant and café

🚇 Ryogoku

♿ Excellent

💴 Moderate

❓ Volunteer guide service for the permanent exhibit (English, Chinese, Korean, French, German, Italian, Spanish, and Russian). Movies, library, good shop

This state-of-the-art museum, opened in 1993, celebrates the history and culture of Tokyo in such a dramatic and interesting way that it merits the reputation as the city's premier history museum.

The building The futuristic sci-fi designed museum was inspired by an old warehouse and reaches a height of 203 feet, about the same height as Edo Castle's topmost tower. The museum covers Tokyo's history from the 17th century to the present.

Earthquakes and aesthetics You enter the permanent exhibition space, spread over two floors, via a reproduction of a wooden Hihombashi bridge, a structure made famous from countless woodblock prints. The area beyond is divided into three sections—History Zone, Edo Zone, and Tokyo Zone. —each filled with diverse displays ranging from business life, the aesthetics of Edo, and urban culture and pleasure. Displays covering civilization and enlightenment are not far from those covering the two great 20th-century disasters to befall the city, the 1923 Kanto earthquake and the firebombing of Tokyo in 1945. Original material and images are included, as well as large-scale models and faithful reproductions. Special interest exhibitions and lectures are regularly held, and an audio-visual hall presenting three-dimensional images of the past. A library on Level 7 is open to the public.

An exhibit at the Edo-Tokyo Museum

ASAKUSA KANNON TEMPLE

Old Japan lives on in the bustling Asakusa quarter. The ceremonies in its temple are more colorful than those in others in Tokyo, and even when nothing much is happening there's a happy crowd here intent on shopping at the many stalls.

The people's favorite Now dedicated to uniting the competing Buddhist factions, the Asakusa Kannon Temple (Sensoji Temple) has its origins in the 7th century. Pilgrims came from all over Japan, and the Asakusa neighborhood set about entertaining them—providing food and lodging, theaters, houses of pleasure, and *onsen* (baths). The area, leveled by earthquakes, bombs, and fires, was always rebuilt to resemble the original and remains a favorite haunt of out-of-town visitors and the foreigners who discover it. Late afternoon is a good time to come, when dozens of food stalls send up tantalizing aromas and circus performers amuse the crowds.

The sights Near the subway station, opposite the Kaminarimon gate entrance to the temple grounds, is the local information center for maps and leaflets. Through the gate is Nakamise-dori, a pedestrian street lined by little shops, which leads to a second gate, Hozomon, with an elegant five-story pagoda. Straight ahead lies the main shrine hall, just beyond a great bronze urn wreathed in incense, which visitors wave over themselves in the belief that it has curative properties. To the right (west) of the temple is Asakusa Jinja, a Shinto shrine. The east gate, Nitenmon, survives largely intact from the year 1618.

HIGHLIGHTS

- Nakamise-dori: little shops
- Hozomon (gate)
- Five-story pagoda
- Worshippers "washing" in smoke
- Main Sensoji Shrine
- Tokinokane Bell
- Denbo-in Temple Garden (➤ 58)
- Chingodo Temple
- Rice-cracker makers
- Clowns and acrobats

INFORMATION

- ✚ N2
- ✉ 2-3-1 Asakusa, Taito-ku
- ☎ 3842–0181
- 🕐 6AM—sunset
- 🍴 The area is noted for good restaurants
- 🚇 Asakusa
- ♿ Good
- 🎫 Free
- ↔ Sumida River cruise (➤ 43), Kappabashi (➤ 61)
- ❓ Included in many city tours

A bronze Buddha in the temple gardens

TOKYO DISNEYLAND

HIGHLIGHTS

- Space Mountain
- Splash Mountain
- It's a Small World
- Star Tours
- "Fantillusion" evening parade
- Fireworks
- Photo opportunities
- Spectacular resort hotels
- Running, dancing cleaners
- Children's faces

INFORMATION

- Off map
- 1-1 Maihama, Urayasu-shi
- 047/354–0001 (English language information)
- Open 9AM. Closing time varies from 7 to 10PM. Closed six days in mid-Jan
- Many restaurants and snack bars
- Urayasu, then bus
- Maihama, (15 minutes from Tokyo Station via Keiyo Line), then free shuttle bus to Disneyland or to the hotel area
- Very good
- Expensive
- Tour companies offer day trips from Tokyo. 40 minutes by shuttle bus from Narita International Airport, Tokyo Station (Yaesu north exit) or Ueno Station (Iriya exit)

The plummet from the summit of Splash Mountain

After nearly 20 years of operation, the Japanese are little diminished in their enthusiasm for this classic theme park. Although the locals are having a great time, their jubilation is not as demonstrative as that of Western visitors.

The park A near replica of the California original, although slightly bigger, the Tokyo version is owned and operated under license by a local company set up by big banks and industrial corporations. It opened in 1983 and was an instant success, with over 10 million visitors in the first year. All the most popular rides and attractions found in other Disney parks are here too. On busy days, mainly weekends and holidays, you may have to stand in line for half an hour for Splash Mountain, Space Mountain, or Star Tours. Midweek, there may be no wait at all. The "cast members" (staff) are utterly committed: see the cleaners' high-speed ballet as they whisk up any trace of litter. And where else do they bow as you get on and off the rides? It isn't the Japanese way to walk around and eat at the same time, so there are fewer snack places than in the U.S. theme parks.

Staying over The five big resort hotels, in the Tokyo Bay area clustered close to Disneyland are all packed with families every weekend, but being near the city and on the way to the airport, they are popular business venues as well.

TOKYO's *best*

ART COLLECTIONS

See Top 25 Sights for
NATIONAL MUSEUM OF MODERN ART (▶ 37)
NATIONAL MUSEUM OF WESTERN ART (▶ 45)

Bridgestone highlights

- *Mlle Georgette Charpentier Seated*, Renoir
- *Saltimbanque Seated with Arms Crossed*, Picasso
- *Windmills on Montmartre*, Van Gogh
- *Self-portrait*, Manet
- *Mont Sainte-Victoire and Château Noir*, Cézanne
- *Still Life with Cat*, Tsuguharu Fujita
- *Faunesse*, Rodin
- *Degas bronzes*
- *Desire*, Maillol

BRIDGESTONE MUSEUM OF ART

The founder of the Bridgestone Tire Company used some of his wealth to buy art. He specialized in the French Impressionists, Post-Impressionists, and Meiji-period Japanese artists who painted in western style. A sculpture collection includes ancient Egyptian, Greek and Roman, as well as 20th-century works.
✚ L6 ✉ 1-10-1 Kyobashi, Chuo-ku (entrance on Yaesu-dori)
☎ 3563–0241 🕐 Tue–Sun 10–5.30. Closed late Dec–early Jan and weeks before and after special exhibitions 🍴 Cafés and restaurants nearby Ⓜ Kyobashi, Nihonbashi 💶 Moderate

HARA MUSEUM OF CONTEMPORARY ART

Displays a large collection of abstract Japananse, U.S., and European art from the 1950s to the present day. Housed in an Art Deco house built by art collector Hara Toshio in 1938, six galleries ranged off long corridors display perfectly the unconventional art. The additional café overlooks pleasant lawns and more outdoor art.
✚ Off map to south ✉ 4-7-25 Kita Shinagawa, Shinagawa-ku
☎ 3445–0651 🕐 Tue–Sun 11–5 🍴 Café Ⓜ Shinagawa
💶 Expensive

Toshusai Sharaku's
Sawamura Sojuro III
in the Role of Kujaku
Saburo *in the Ota
Memorial Museum
of Art*

IDEMITSU MUSEUM OF ARTS

The Asian art on display here—including calligraphy, painting, and ceramics is superb. Two 16th-century screens—one of cherry blossoms, the other of colorful kimonos—show that Japanese reverence for these subjects is nothing new. The collection, formed by oil industry magnate Sazo Idemitsu (1885–1981), is so vast that only a tiny fraction can be shown at one time. One room is devoted to the odd but fascinating archive of potsherds of the world. Check out the great view of central Tokyo from the museum's windows.
✚ K6 ✉ Kokusai Building 9F, 3-1-1 Marunouchi, Chiyoda-ku
☎ 3213–9402 🕐 Tue–Sun 10–5. Closed Dec 29–Jan 3 🍴 Free tea
Ⓜ Yurakucho 💶 Moderate

NEZU INSTITUTE OF FINE ARTS

Located in the smart area of Aoyama, the Institute is a treasury of Japanese, Chinese, and Korean fine arts collected by buisnessman Nezu Kaichiro, who died in 1940. The gallery is in its own beautiful gardens, several with tea ceremony pavilions.
✚ F8 ✉ 6-5-1 Minami-Aoyama, Minato-ku ☎ 3400–2536
🕐 Tue–Sun 9:30–4:30. Closed day after national holidays 🍴 Nearby snack bar and restaurants Ⓜ Omotesando (10-minute walk)
💶 Expensive

OTA MEMORIAL MUSEUM

At this museum, you have to exchange your shoes for slippers. The *ukiyo-e* prints (see panel opposite), and the original paintings from which they were made, were collected by business magnate Seizo Ota (1893–1977). He amassed 10,000 examples, and the museum has since acquired more, so the displays are frequently rotated.

⊞ E7 ✉ 1-10-10 Jingumae, Shibuya-ku ☎ 3403–0880 ◷ Tue–Sun 10:30–5:30. Closed from 26th to end of each month and Dec 19–Jan 2 ⊩ Drinks and snacks in basement ◨ Meijijingu-mae ⊠ Harajuku (JR) ◕ Moderate

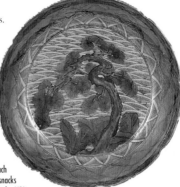

A ceramic dish with a pine tree design in the collection of the Suntory Museum

SEIJI TOGO MEMORIAL ART MUSEUM

Many of the paintings on show here are by Seiji Togo (1897–1978), whose work depicts the grace and beauty of Japanese women. The museum made headlines when it paid a world-record price for Van Gogh's *Sunflowers* in 1987, and is noted for its 33 pictures by the American primitive, Grandma Moses.

⊞ C4 ✉ Yasuda Kasai Kaijo Building 42F, 1-26-1 Nishi-Shinjuku, Shinjuku-ku ☎ 3349–3081 ◷ Tue–Sun 9:30–4:30. Closed Dec 27–Jan 4 ⊩ Restaurants in same building ◨ ⊠ Shinjuku ◕ Moderate

SUNTORY MUSEUM

The famous whiskey company is a great patron of the arts. This museum houses a small but beautiful display of some of the best of Japanese traditional art in rotating exhibitions of paintings, ceramics, lacquerware, textiles, and carvings from the museum's own collection, or on loan.

⊞ G6 ✉ Suntory Building 11F, 1-2-3 Moto-Akasaka, Minato-ku ☎ 3470–1073 ◷ Tue–Thu, Sat–Sun 10–4:30; Fri 10–7 ⊩ Tea house; restaurants in same building ◨ Akasaka-mitsuke ◕ Moderate

TOKYO METROPOLITAN ART MUSEUM

The spacious galleries here accommodate touring exhibitions and modern art shows. There is also a small permanent collection of 20th-century Japanese art, mostly in western styles.

⊞ L1 ✉ Ueno Park, Taito-ku ☎ 3821–3726 ◷ Tue–Sun 9–4 ⊩ Café ◨ Ueno ◕ Free (except special exhibitions)

WATARI MUSEUM OF CONTEMPORARY ART

This small gallery specializes in cutting-edge art with new exhibitions every few months. The gift shop sells sketchbooks, photo albums, a huge selection of art postcards, and arty T-shirts.

⊞ E7 ✉ 3-7-6 Jingumae, Shibuya-ku ☎ 3402–3001 ◷ Tue–Sun 11–7 ⊩ Café ◨ Gaienmae ◕ Expensive

Ukiyo-e

Woodblock prints (*ukiyo-e*) were art for the common people, depicting views, beautiful women, and *kabuki* actors. They were highly popular beginning about 1700, and new designs are still being produced today. Among the greatest names, Katsushika Hokusai (1760–1849), painter of the *The 36 Views of Mount Fuji*, and Utagawa Hiroshige (1797–1858) are well known internationally. Early prints in fine condition are worth fortunes, and even modern hand-colored copies can be expensive. These days, color-laser copies make a convincing substitute.

MUSEUMS

Oh Yoko!

The John Lennon Museum presents an account of the life of the brilliant ex-Beatle through the somewhat biased eyes of his Japanese wife Yoko Ono. Displays, arranged chronologically, include artworks, photographs, original song manuscripts, clothes, and musical instruments. His best music is featured on speakers and headphones. The poignant final room presents his words in respectful silence.

➕ Off map to north
✉ Saitama New Urban Center
☎ 048–601–0009
🕓 Wed–Mon 11–6
🍴 Nearby
🚇 Saitama Shin-Toshin on JR Keihin line
💰 Expensive

See Top 25 Sights for
EDO-TOKYO MUSEUM (➤ 48)
JAPANESE SWORD MUSEUM (➤ 29)
TOKYO NATIONAL MUSEUM (➤ 46)

FUKAGAWA EDO MUSEUM

A faithfully reproduced collection of 19th-century Tokyo buildings from a riverside district, all contained within the museum and featuring state-of-the-art display technology.

➕ N5 ✉ 1-3-28 Shirakawa, Koto-ku ☎ 3630–8625 🕓 Daily 9:30–5; Sat, Sun 10–6. Closed Dec 28–Jan 5 and second and fourth Mon 🍴 Nearby 🚇 Kiyosumi-Shirakawa 💰 Moderate

MUSEUM OF MARITIME SCIENCE

Designed to resemble a concrete ship, this museum of ships and sailing is sited on an island in Tokyo Bay. Historic vessels are moored nearby.

➕ Off map in Tokyo Bay ✉ 3-1 Higashi-Yashio, Shinagawa-ku ☎ 5500–1111 🕓 Mon–Fri 10–5; Sat, Sun 10–6. National holidays 10–6. Closed Dec 28–31 🍴 Restaurant and snack bar 🚇 Fune-no-kagakukan (from Shinbashi via Yurikamome monorail) 🚤 River bus from Hinode Pier (K8) 💰 Moderate

TOKYO METROPOLITAN MUSEUM OF PHOTOGRAPHY

The museum is part of the 1990s Yebisu Garden Place development (➤ 32). Early photographs on show include some from before the Meiji Restoration of 1868, recording daily life of the time. Imaginative displays demonstrate time-honored optical illusions and their modern equivalent, holography.

A gallery in the Museum of Photography

➕ E10 ✉ 1-13-3 Mita, Meguro-ku ☎ 3280–0031 🕓 Tue–Thu, Sat–Sun 10–6; Fri 10–9. Closed Tue if Mon is a national holiday and Dec 28–Jan 4 🍴 Coffee shop 🚇 Ebisu 💰 Expensive

SHITAMACHI MUSEUM

A compact museum recording working-class life of a century ago. Check out the merchant's shop, candy store, and coppersmith's home. You can handle everyday objects and view early photographs.

➕ L2 ✉ 2-1 Ueno Koen, Taito-ku ☎ 3823–7451 🕓 Tue–Sun 9:30–5 🍴 Snack bar 🚇 Ueno 💰 Inexpensive

VIEWS FROM THE TOP

See Top 25 Sights for
METROPOLITAN GOVERNMENT OFFICES (▶ 26)
TOKYO TOWER (▶ 34)

AKASAKA PRINCE

The hotel stands on a central hilltop site, so the bar and restaurant on the top of its 40 stories have the city's best view of Akasaka, the Imperial Palace, Ginza, and Tokyo Bay.

➕ H6 ✉ 1-2 Kioi-cho, Chiyoda-ku ☎ 3234–1111 🕐 Daily 11:30AM–midnight 🍴 Bar and restaurant 🚇 Nagatacho

KEIO PLAZA HOTEL 47TH FLOOR

The rooftop of the first skyscraper to be built in Shinjuku is a spectacular vantage point. At night, the window seats in the hotel's penthouse cocktail bars wouldn't suit sufferers from vertigo, and the prices are similarly elevated.

➕ D4 ✉ 2-2-1 Nishi-Shinjuku, Shinjuku-ku ☎ 3344–0111 🕐 Daily 10–6 🍴 Snacks, plus many restaurants in hotel 🚇 Shinjuku 🕴 Moderate

SUMITOMO TOWER

This 52-story, six-sided building with a hollow center has a lookout point, and the top three floors are given over to restaurants used by office workers at lunchtime, some of which stay open in the evening. Window tables have the kind of view you might get from a spaceship.

➕ D4 ✉ 2-6-1 Nishi-Shinjuku, Shinjuku-ku 🕐 Daily 9AM–10PM 🍴 Many restaurants 🚇 Shinjuku 🕴 Free

SUNSHINE 60 OBSERVATORY

One of the world's fastest elevators carries you to the 60th floor in under a minute. Choose a clear day: when the smog is bad, you can see only the local area. The same huge complex also houses the Ancient Orient Museum and a planetarium. An aquarium on the 11th floor is home to 20,000 fish of over 600 species, a coral reef, snowy penguin habitat, and outdoor marine garden. The seawater for the tanks comes from Tokyo Bay.

➕ Off map ✉ Sunshine City, 3-1-3 Higashi-Ikebukuro, Toshima-ku ☎ 3989–3331 🕐 Jul 21–Aug 31: daily 10–8:30. Sep1 –Jul 20: Mon–Sat 10–6; Sun and national holidays 10–6:30 🍴 Restaurants and snack bars 🚇 Higashi-Ikebukuro 🕴 Expensive

WESTIN TOKYO HOTEL

The 22nd-floor bar and restaurant here, and the top of Yebisu in the same complex, look out on the Yebisu Garden Place (▶ 32), north to Shibuya, and east to Shinagawa and the bay.

➕ E10 ✉ Yebisu Garden Place, 1-4-1 Mita, Meguro-ku ☎ 5423–7000 🕐 Daily 11AM–midnight 🍴 Bar and restaurant 🚇 Ebisu

An aerial view of the skyscrapers of Shinjuku

Ikebukuro

One of Tokyo's most interesting growth areas, and easy to reach by several subway lines and JR's Yamanote loop between Shinjuku and Ueno, Ikebukuro is one of the city's livliest places. Once a working-class district, big business has planted a few enormous buildings and the city's largest department stores, including the huge Seibu, trendy Parco, and the amazing Tokyu Hands DIY store (▶ 76). Toyota's Amlux showroom (▶ 60) is across the street from Sunshine 60.

SHRINES & TEMPLES

Shinto

Most Japanese are to some extent followers of Shinto, which they call *Kami-no-Michi*, meaning "the Way of the Gods (or Spirits)." Originating as a belief in the spirits of nature, it places great emphasis on purity of conduct, mind and motive, and corresponding physical cleanliness. A Shinto shrine (*jinja* or *jingu*) is marked by its *torii* gate or gates, shaped like a giant perch for the mythical cock which crowed and brought the sun goddess Amaterasu out of her cave to light up the world.

Shrine workers at Hie Jinja

HANAZONO SHRINE

Now surrounded by the monuments of commerce and pleasure, this is one of the oldest shrines in Tokyo. People pray here for success in business.
⊞ E4 ⊠ Opposite Marui Interior store, Shinjuku Sanchome, Shinjuku-ku ⏰ Sunrise–9PM 🍴 Plenty nearby 🚇 Shinjuku Sanchome 💰 Free

HIE JINJA

One of Tokyo's most picturesque shrines is opposite the main entrance to the Capitol Tokyu Hotel, up a steep flight of stairs. You will notice statues of monkeys carrying their young: one of the deities enshrined here is believed to protect women against miscarriages. Hie Jinja was a favorite of the *shogun*s and the site of Edo's greatest religious festival.
⊞ H6 ⊠ 2-10-5 Nagatacho, Chiyoda-ku ☎ 3581–2471 ⏰ Sunrise–sunset 🚇 Kokkaigijido-mae 💰 Free

KANDA MYOJIN SHRINE

One of Tokyo's oldest foundations and the focus of the Kanda Festival, held in alternate years in May. The festival's highlight is a procession of dozens of portable shrines. The present shrine buildings are replicas of those destroyed in the earthquake and fires of 1923. On Sundays, young couples come to have their weddings blessed, the brides gorgeously arrayed in their most expensive kimono.
⊞ K3 ⊠ 2-16-2 Soto-Kanda, Chiyoda-ku ☎ 3254–0753 ⏰ Sunrise–sunset 🚇 Ochanomizu 💰 Free

KIYOMIZU KANNON

Bullet holes in the Kuromon gate date from the 1868 battle for the hill. Childless women pray to a Kannon figure in the shrine, and, if they subsequently have a baby, return to leave a doll in gratitude and to pray for the child's good health. Every September 25 the accumulated dolls are burned in a great bonfire.
⊞ L2 ⊠ Ueno Koen, Taito-ku ⏰ Sunrise–sunset 🍴 Plenty nearby 🚇 Ueno 💰 Free

SOGENJI TEMPLE

Close to the Kappabashi shops (► 61), this is also known as Kappa Temple, a name derived from the legendary water sprites who helped to drain the marshes that once covered this area.
⊞ M1 ⊠ 3-7-2 Matsuya, Taito-ku ☎ 3841–2035 ⏰ Sunrise–sunset 🚇 Iriya 💰 Free

Bronze lanterns line the path to Toshogu Shrine

SUMIYOSHI SHRINE

Fishermen were brought to this island in the Sumida River from Osaka by Ieyasu Tokugawa to set up a fishing industry. It was they who built this shrine to the god who protects them when they are at sea.

🚇 M7 ✉ 1-1 Tsukuda, Chuo-ku ☎ 3531-3500 🕐 Sunrise–sunset 🚇 Tsukishima 🎫 Free

TOGO SHRINE

Set amid gardens and overlooking a lake, the shrine is a tribute to Admiral Togo, Japan's naval hero in the 1905 destruction of the Russian fleet at Tsushima. Tokyo's largest antiques market is held here on the 1st, 4th, and 5th Sundays of the month.

🚇 E6 ✉ Off Meiji-dori, Harajuku, Shibuya-ku ☎ 3403–3591 🕐 Sunrise–sunset 🚇 Meijijingu-mae 🎫 Free

TOSHOGU SHRINE

This shrine, dating from 1651, is dedicated to the first Tokugawa *shogun*, Ieyasu, who died in 1616 and was quickly proclaimed divine. One of few vestiges of the early Edo period, it somehow escaped destruction in the 1868 battle between adherents of the emperor and those of the Tokugawas, when most buildings on Ueno hill were burned down. The path from the *torii* is lined by over 200 stone and bronze lanterns.

🚇 L2 ✉ 9-88 Ueno Koen, Taito-ku ☎ 3822–3455 🕐 9:30–4:30 🍴 Food stands nearby 🚇 Ueno 🎫 Moderate

YUSHIMA SEIDO

This shrine was founded in the 17th century for the study of Confucianism, not strictly a religion, more a philosophy and code of conduct. The shrine building is unusually austere. The first training institute for teachers was set up here in 1872, and in due course it evolved into Tokyo University.

🚇 K3 ✉ 1-4-25 Yushima, Bunkyo-ku ☎ 3251–4606 🕐 9:30–4 🚇 Ochanomizu 🎫 Free

Shrine etiquette

Japanese who visit a shrine go through elaborate rituals upon entering. Tourists need only to dress respectably, although short sleeves and shorts are acceptable—use discretion. The rituals are:

- Pass under the *torii* (gate)
- Wash hands thoroughly in the stone basin
- With the dipper, pour water into a cupped hand and rinse the mouth
- Approach the shrine and throw coins into the offertory box
- Bow deeply twice
- Clap hands twice (or pull the bell rope)
- Bow once more

PARKS & GARDENS

The scenic Rikugien Garden

Landscape in miniature

The Korakuen garden was laid out in the 17th century by a refugee from Ming Dynasty China who scattered it with tiny replicas of famous Chinese lakes, rivers, and mountains. The miniature landscape even extends to growing a small field of rice, duly harvested in October. There's a collection of bridges, ranging from simple stepping stones to the Full Moon Bridge, a half circle of stone that, with its reflection, forms a perfect O. The huge weeping cherry tree near the gate was near to dying some years ago, unable to blossom. It was saved by the botanical version of a heart transplant: new roots were grafted onto it.

> **See Top 25 Sights for**
> **HAMA RIKYU GARDEN (► 43)**
> **HIBIYA PARK (► 40)**
> **IMPERIAL PALACE EAST GARDEN (► 36)**
> **IRIS GARDEN, MEIJI SHRINE (► 30)**
> **SHINJUKU NATIONAL GARDEN (► 28)**

DENBO-IN TEMPLE GARDEN

Entry to the lovely private garden of the temple is by ticket only (collect from the office next to the Asakusa pagoda ► 49). The garden is reached by the temple's side gate (facing Denboin-dori, opposite Asakusa Public Hall). It was designed in the early 17th century by the tea ceremony master Enshu Kobori. The garden pond, with resident carp and turtles, beautifully reflects the abbot's quarters and more distant pagoda.
✚ N2 ✉ Asakusa, Taito-ku ◉ Mon–Fri 10–2:30 🍴 Plenty nearby 🚇 Asakusa 💷 Free

KIYOSUMI GARDEN

Across the Sumida River opposite the Tokyo City Air Terminal, this is an oddity. A pond stocked with 10,000 carp is surrounded by many and varied rocks brought from all over Japan.
✚ N5–N6 ✉ 3-3-9 Kiyosumi, Koto-ku ☎ 3641–5892 ◉ Daily 9–4:30 🚇 Morishita 💷 Moderate

KOISHIKAWA KORAKUEN GARDEN

Tokyo's oldest garden was laid out in the 17th century for one of the Tokugawa family, a relative of the *shogun*. Over the years, it was reduced to a quarter of the original size, and all the buildings—tea houses, gates and shrines—were destroyed in World War II. Now

restored, it's a sanctuary for office workers with their
lunch boxes, and housewives seeking some space.
🔲 J3 ✉ 1-6-6 Koraku, Bunkyo-ku ☎ 3811–3015 🕐 Tue–Sun
9–5. Closed Tue if Mon is a national holiday or Dec 29–Jan 3
🍴 Plenty nearby 🚉 Suidobashi 🎫 Moderate

NEW OTANI HOTEL GARDEN
Next to the giant hotel is a fine traditional Japanese
garden with streams and lily ponds, decorative
bridges, and manicured shrubs. It continues the
tradition of an early Edo-period garden on this site.
🔲 G5 ✉ 4-1 Kioi-cho, Chiyoda-ku ☎ 3265–1111 🕐 Daily 9–9
🍴 In hotel 🚉 Yotsuya 🎫 Moderate (free for hotel guests)

RIKUGIEN GARDEN
Widely regarded as the city's most beautiful Japanese
garden, Rikugien was laid out in 1695 for a patron
with literary tastes: the name means "six poem
garden," and each of its scenic features was inspired
by a poetic reference. Cloistered away from the noise
of the city by a high brick wall, this is landscaped art
of a high order, entirely artificial yet seeming natural.
🔲 Off map to north ✉ 6-16-3 Honkomagomae, Bunkyo-ku
☎ 3491–2222 🕐 Tue–Sun 9–5. Closed Dec 29–Jan 3 🚉 Sengoku,
Sugamo (Toei Mita Line) 🎫 Moderate

UENO PARK
The park is the home of several museums, concert
halls, and a zoo (▶ 62). Some of Tokyo's homeless
sleep out in the open here, even in the coldest
weather. In spring, locals come in their thousands to
admire the cherry blossoms. Check
out the ducks and geese on Shinobazu
Pond, where species from the Arctic
and Siberia spend the winter.
🔲 L1–L2 ✉ Ueno Koen, Taito-ku 🕐 Tue–Sun
sunrise–sunset. Closed Tue if Mon is a national
holiday) 🍴 Restaurants and food stands
🚉 Ueno 🚉 Ueno JR (Park exit more convenient
than subway) 🎫 Free (museums, shrines, and the
zoo charge entry fees)

YOYOGI PARK
Once an imperial army training
ground, then renamed Washington Heights by the
U.S. occupation forces who used it for housing, the
area became the site of the 1964 Olympic village and
was renamed Yoyogi Park. The park's paths, lawns,
and wooded areas are pleasant to stroll through. The
Yoyogi Sports Center, just across the road, was also
created for the Games. Its stadium's pillarless roof is
still strikingly modern.
🔲 D6 ✉ Yoyogi, Shibuya-ku 🕐 5AM–5PM 🍴 Snacks
🚉 Meijijingu-mae, Harajuku 🎫 Free

Japanese gardens
Japanese gardens generally come
in three types, although larger
gardens can contain the elements
of more than one. **Hill gardens**,
with miniature hills and a pond or
stream, an island, bridges, and a
meandering path, imitate nature
and may allude to famous beauty
spots without actually mimicking
them. **Flat gardens** have few
plants: rocks, raked gravel, and
sand are designed to aid
contemplation. **Tea gardens**,
next to a tea house, have flowing
lines to contrast with the tea
house's austere simplicity.

*The boating lake near
Ueno Park*

59

HIGH-TECH WIZARDRY

Inside Toyota's Amlux building

Market leader

Since the 1960s, Japan has been first in the field of consumer electronics, almost monopolizing every new invention—color TV, digital cameras, video recorders, microwave ovens, mobile phones, personal computers—for a few years while high profits can be made. Then, as the rest of the world catches up and prices fall, lower-cost manufacturers in Korea, Taiwan and China, Malaysia and Thailand take over while Japan moves on to the next miracle product.

> **See Top 25 Sights for**
> **METROPOLITAN GOVERNMENT OFFICES (➤ 26)**
> **SONY CENTER (➤ 42)**

FUJITA VENTÉ

The latest electronic and video games, including virtual reality, can be tried out here. The building is also a venue for art and architecture exhibitions.

🏙 D5 ✉ Fujita Building BF, 1F and 2F, 4-6-15 Sendagaya, Shibuya-ku ☎ 3796–2486 🕐 Fri–Wed 10–6. Closed Dec 26–Jan 3 🍴 Snacks 🚉 Yoyogi 💷 Free (except special exhibitions)

MEGA WEB

There are three parts to this Tokyo Bay Area complex. Tokyo City Showcase gives you an overview of automobile manufacturing and displays latest models; History Garage features cars from 1950s to 1970s; and Future World displays state-of-the-art transportation systems and a 3D Ride Coaster, a movie synchronized to moving chairs.

🏙 Off map to south ✉ Palette town, 1 Aomi, Koto-ku ☎ 3599–0808 🕐 Daily 11–9 🚉 Aomi station on Yurikamome line 🍴 Cafés 💷 Free entry, rides moderate

NEC SHOWROOM

This is a hands-on exhibition of current model computers and communications technology.

🏙 J6 ✉ C Plaza, Hibiya Kokusai Building B1F, Hibiya City, 2-2-3 Uchisaiwaicho, Chiyoda-ku ☎ 3595–0511 🕐 Mon–Fri 10–6. Closed national holidays 🚉 Uchisaiwaicho 💷 Free

NTT INTERCOMMUNICATION CENTER

Science and art converge in this exhibition and interactive display of computer graphics. The "cave" filled with modifiable 3D imagery is most spectacular.

🏙 C4 ✉ Tokyo Opera City Tower 4F, 3-20-2 Nishi-Shinjuku, Shinjuku-ku ☎ 0120–144199 (toll-free) 🕐 Tue–Thu, Sat–Sun 10–6; Fri 10–9 🍴 Restaurants 53F, 54F 🚉 Hatsudai 💷 Moderate

TEPCO ELECTRIC ENERGY MUSEUM

This museum run by the Tokyo Electric Power Company has seven floors of interactive exhibits.

🏙 D7 ✉ 1-12-10 Jinnan, Shibuya-ku ☎ 3477-1191 🕐 Thu–Tue 10–6 🚉 Shibuya 💷 Free

TOYOTA AUTO SALON AMLUX

In this futuristic blue steel and glass tower, you can climb into every car currently produced by Toyota, inspect the winners of famous rallies, and learn about the latest technical wizardry.

🏙 Off map ✉ 3-3-5 Higashi-Ikebukuro, Toshima-ku ☎ 5391–5900 🕐 Tue–Sat 11–8; Sun, national holidays 10–7:30. Closed Tue if Mon is a national holiday 🍴 Restaurant and snack bar 🚉 Higashi-Ikebukuro 🚉 Ikebukuro (7-minute walk) 💷 Free

WHAT'S FREE

BEER MUSEUM

This is part of Yebisu Garden Place (➤ 32), reached by moving walkways from Ebisu JR Station. The Sapporo brewery here closed down; today you see the brewing process via virtual reality headsets. The museum's collection of advertising posters includes a gauze-clad beauty of 1908, showing that sex as an aid to sales is no new idea.

➕ E10 ✉ 4-20-1 Ebisu, Shibuya-ku ☎ 5423–7255 🕐 Tue–Sun 10–6. Closed Mon and Dec 28–Jan 4 🍴 Huge beer hall, restaurants, and fast-food outlets 🚉 Ebisu 🎫 Free

KAPPABASHI

What Tsukiji is to fish, Kappabashi is to plates, pans, chopsticks, knives, lanterns, signs, and everything the massive restaurant business needs except food —the stores here sell only the plastic variety. A huge head crowned with a chef's hat stands on top of a tall building to mark the beginning of Kappabashi-dori.

➕ M2 ✉ Kappabashi-dori, Taito-ku 🕐 Shops: Mon–Sat 9:30–6:30 approx. 🍴 Wide choice 🚉 Tawaramachi 🎫 Free

MEGURO PARASITOLOGICAL MUSEUM

A popular date spot, this unusual museum is not for the queasy. The highlight is an 26-foot tapeworm.

➕ Off map ✉ 4-1-1 Shimo-Meguro, Meguro-ku ☎ 3716–1264 🕐 Tue–Sun 10–5 🚉 Meguro 🎫 Free

ORIGAMI KAIKAN

You can watch work going on in the factory and demonstrations of *origami*, the art of paper folding. Special papers and paper crafts are sold in the shop.

➕ K3 ✉ 1-7-14 Yushima, Bunkyo-ku ☎ 3811–4025 🕐 Mon–Sat 9–5. Closed national holidays 🍴 Snacks nearby 🚉 Ochanomizu (5-minute walk) 🎫 Free

SUMO MUSEUM

A store of records, relics, and pictures of past *yokozuna*—the grand masters of *sumo* wrestling—is housed in the building which is also the main venue for matches. You may see some of today's big men arriving in their stretch limousines.

➕ N4 ✉ 1-3-28 Yokoami, Sumida-ku ☎ 3622–0366 🕐 Daily 9:30–4:30. Closed during tournaments, except to ticket holders 🍴 Snacks 🚉 Ryogoku 🎫 Free

Model menus

Japan's famous food replicas are much appreciated by every visitor who can't speak Japanese or read a menu. The models, *sampuru*, were first devised in the 19th century to show what new foods introduced from abroad looked like, and before plastic they were made of painted plaster and gelatine. Shopkeepers were surprised when foreigners wanted to buy them, but soon adapted to the market opportunity. Realistic replicas are not cheap—a plate of plastic noodles can cost a lot more than the real thing.

Advertising posters in the Beer Museum

FOR KIDS

See Top 25 Sights for
SONY CENTER (► 42)
TOKYO DISNEYLAND (► 50)
TOKYO JOYPOLIS (► 47)

Toshima-en

This elaborate amusement park in a northwestern suburb has some of the wildest roller-coaster rides, loops, corkscrews, and spins anywhere, including a long freefall. There are also plenty of gentler rides to suit smaller children as well as a waterpark with several pools and slides.

🚩 Off map ✉ 3-25-1 Koyama, Nerima-ku ☎ 3990–3131 🕐 Wed–Mon 10–5 🍴 Snacks and fast food 🚇 Toshima-en (Seibu-Ikebukuro Line) 💰 Expensive

HANAYASHIKI

This amusement park was founded in 1853. The rides, intended primarily for children, include carousels, bumper cars, and a haunted house.
🚩 N2 ✉ 2-28-1 Asakusa, Taito-ku ☎ 3842–8780 🕐 Wed–Mon 10–6. OpenTue during school holidays 🍴 Snacks 🚇 Asakusa 💰 Expensive

KORAKUEN

This fairground and amusement park has a giant roller-coaster, the Ultra Twister, and loop-the-loop train, as well as gentler rides for younger children. The entry ticket does not include the cost of rides.
🚩 J3 ✉ 1-3-61 Koraku, Bunkyo-ku ☎ 3811-2111 🕐 Daily 10–6 🍴 Snack bars and food stands 🚇 Korakuen, Suidobashi 🚇 Suidobashi 💰 Expensive

NHK BROADCASTING CENTER

NHK runs tours of the sets used for their TV programs. Performances are in Japanese.
🚩 D7 ✉ 2-2-1 Jinnan, Shibuya-ku ☎ 3485–8034 🕐 Tue–Sun 10–6. Closed Tue if Mon is a natioal holiday 🍴 Snacks 🚇 Meijijingu-mae 🚇 Shibuya 💰 Moderate

SHINAGAWA AQUARIUM

A well-stocked aquarium with a walk-through glass tunnel, so you can feel surrounded by sharks. Shows by performing sea lions and dolphins run four or five times daily.
🚩 Off map ✉ 3-2-1 Katsushima, Shinagawa-ku ☎ 3762–3431 🕐 Wed –Mon 10–5. Closed Dec29–Jan 1 🍴 Snacks 🚇 Omorikaigan (Keihin-Kyuko Line from Shinagawa) 💰 Moderate

TSUKUDA TOY MUSEUM

Tokyo's best toy museum displays a collection of over 8,000 post-Meji era toys.
🚩 N2 ✉ 1-36-10 Hashiba, Asakusa ☎ 3874–5133 🕐 Tue–Sun 9:30–5 🍴 Nearby 🚇 Asakusa 💰 Moderate

UENO ZOO

Japan's first zoo, which opened in Ueno Park in the late 19th century, displays over 350 species including the popular giant pandas, which are fed daily at 3:30. They're not on view on a Friday. There is an open-air section where children can stroke the animals.
🚩 L1 ✉ Ueno Park ☎ 3828–5171 🕐 Tue–Sun 9:30–5 🍴 Café 🚇 Ueno JR 💰 Moderate

Young visitors can view the underwater acrobatics of Shinagawa Aquarium's sealife from a glass tunnel

TOKYO
where to...

JAPANESE RESTAURANTS

Prices

Price guides for Japanese restaurants (▶ 64–6) are for set menus, known as "*setto*"; most restaurants offer a choice of these. Lunch sets generally cost much less than dinner.

$ up to ¥3,000

$$ ¥3,000–¥8,000

$$$ over ¥8,000

Choices

Bento: Box lunch.

Kaiseki ryori: Refined cuisine of many small delicacies, using typically Japanese ingredients.

Kushiage: Deep-fried morsels on sticks.

Miso: Soybean paste.

Ramen: Chinese noodles, in soups, usually with pork.

Robatayaki: Food cooked over a charcoal grill.

Shabu-shabu: Thin slices of beef swirled in a boiling broth, then dipped in sauces.

Soba: Buckwheat noodles.

Sukiyaki: Thinly sliced beef cooked at the table with vegetables and *tofu*.

Teishoku: Fixed-price menu.

Tempura: Shrimps, fish, and vegetables coated in light batter and deep fried.

Teppanyaki: Fish, meat, and vegetables cooked on a griddle.

Udon: Wheat-flour noodles.

Yakitori: Small pieces of chicken, liver, or other meat, grilled on bamboo skewers.

FUROSATO ($$)

Traditional country food in a picturesque old mountain farmhouse reconstructed here. Fish, chicken, and vegetables grilled over a *hibachi* (small charcoal grill) are a specialty.
✚ D9 ✉ 3-4-1 Aobadai, Meguro-ku ☎ 3463–2310 ⏰ Daily 5–11 Ⓜ Nakameguro Ⓡ Shibuya

FUTABA ($)

Ueno is known especially for *tonkatsu*, fried pork cutlet, eaten with rice, soup, and pickled vegetables; this is one of the oldest restaurants serving it.
✚ L2 ✉ 2-8-11 Ueno, Taito-ku ☎ 3831–6483 ⏰ Daily 11:30–2:30, 5–7:30 Ⓜ Ueno

GOMBEI ($)

With its abrupt service, this place is perfect if you are tired of being polite—and want some of the best noodles to be found in town.
✚ E7 ✉ 5-9-3 Minami-Aoyama, Minato-ku ☎ 3406–5733 ⏰ Daily 11–11 Ⓜ Omotesando

HASSAN ($$)

A busy traditional restaurant with a choice of seating on chairs or on *tatami* (straw mats). The set tempura, sukiyaki, and *shabu-shabu* menus include all-you-can-eat options, at a higher price.
✚ G8 ✉ Denki Building B1F, 6-1-20 Roppongi, Minato-ku ☎ 3403–8333 ⏰ Daily 11:30–2, 5–11 Ⓜ Roppongi

HAYASHI ($$)

Kimono-clad women oversee the *hibachi* cooking operations.
✚ D4 ✉ Hide Building, 2-22-5 Kabuki-cho, Shinjuku ☎ 3209–5672 Ⓜ Mon–Sat 5–11:30 Ⓡ Shinjuku

IZU'EI ($$)

Traditionally decorated, specializing in charcoal-grill, tempura, and sushi as well as set meals. There's no English menu, but the menu has some pictures.
✚ L2 ✉ 2-12-22 Shinobazu, Ueno ☎ 38310954 ⏰ Daily 11ᴀᴍ–9:30ᴘᴍ Ⓜ Ueno JR

KUREMUTSU ($$)

The specialties in this traditional house with a delightful courtyard, are grilled fish, sashimi, and *kaiseki* meals. Reservations essential.
✚ N2 ✉ 2-2-13 Asakus Walk, Nakamise ☎ 3842–0906 ⏰ Fri–Wed 4–9:30 Ⓜ Asakusa

MUNAKATA ($$)

Try the cheaper lunchtime meals at this intimate and popular *kaiseki* (haute cuisine) restaurant. Good boxed lunches.
✚ K7 ✉ Mitsui Urban Hotel basemen, 8-6-15 Ginza, Chou-ku ☎ 3574–9356 Ⓜ Mon–Fri 11:30–3, 5–10; Sat, Sun and hols 11:30–10 Ⓜ Shinbashi or Hibiya

MYOKO ($)

The house specialty is *hoto* (wide, flat *udon*). Try the hot *hoto nabe* with miso broth and vegetables.
✚ D8 ✉ Shinto Building 1F, 1-17-2 Shibuya, Shibuya-ku ☎ 3499–3450 ⏰ Daily 11–10 Ⓡ Shibuya

NAKASE ($$$)

A famous and long-established tempura restaurant near Nakamise-dori. Follow your nose and be prepared to wait. Often the line forms well before opening time. Lunch is best—for economy and because the area shuts down early in the evening.

🚇 N2 ✉ 1-39-13 Asakusa, Taito-ku ☎ 3841–4015 🕐 Wed–Mon noon–8 🚇 Asakusa

NOBU ($$$)

Reservations are essential at this classy restaurant where friendly waiters serve contemporary Japanese cuisine with efficiency. Sushi and sashimi on the menu (and the sushi rolls are renowned). Or try the spicy sour shrimp or the black cod with miso.

🚇 E8 ✉ 6-10-17 Minami Aoyama, Minato-ku ☎ 5467–0022 🕐 Mon–Fri 11:30–2; daily 6–10 🚇 Shibuya or Omotesando

SHABU ZEN ($$)

A big restaurant special-izing in *shabu-shabu*, and including all-you-can-eat deals. The American beef is less costly than the local.

🚇 G8 ✉ Three Stars Mansion, 5-17-16 Roppongi, Minato-ku ☎ 3585–5600 🕐 Daily 5PM–11:30PM 🚇 Roppongi

Also at:
🚇 K7 ✉ Ginza Core Building, 5-8-20 Ginza, Chuo-ku 🚇 Higashi-Ginza

TATSUMIYA ($$)

Ryotei cuisine—delicacies in several courses—at an affordable price.

🚇 N2 ✉ 1-33-5 Asakusa, Taito-ku ☎ 3251-0287 🕐 Tue–Sun 12–2, 5–10 🚇 Asakusa

TORIGIN ($)

Traditional yakitori is easy to order from the English menu in this bustling eatery not far from the Sony Building. Order *kamameshi* (rice with vegetables and other toppings) and miso soup on the side.

🚇 K6 ✉ 5-5-7 Ginza, Chuo-ku ☎ 3571-3333 🕐 Daily 11:30-9:30 🚇 Ginza

TSUKIJI ($$)

A bright and busy all-day restaurant in the heart of Ginza. Often crowded. The set menus at lunchtime are attractive and reasonably priced.

🚇 K7 ✉ Miyuki Building B1F, 5-6-12 Ginza, Chuo-ku ☎ 3571–0071 🕐 Daily 8:30–7 🚇 Higashi-Ginza

TSUNAHACHI ($)

Fine tempura at a surprisingly fair price, but stick to the set menus.

🚇 D4 ✉ 3-31-8 Shinjuku, Shinjuku-ku ☎ 3352–1011 🕐 Daily 11–2, 5–9 🚇 Shinjuku-Sanchome

YABU SOBA ($)

One of Tokyo's most famous *soba* shops, located in an old Japanese house so popular you may have to wait in line.

🚇 K4 ✉ 2-10 Kanda-Awajicho, Chiyoda-ku ☎ 3251–0287 🕐 Tue–Sun 11:30–7 🚇 Awajicho

Etiquette

After wiping your fingers on the moist towel (*oshibori*) brought before your meal, roll it up and keep it for use as a napkin.

Drink soup from the bowl as if it were a cup. Pick out solid pieces with chopsticks. Slurping soup and noodles is considered acceptable and normal.

To eat rice hold the bowl close to your mouth and use chopsticks. Don't point with chopsticks, or lick the ends, or put the ends that go in your mouth into a communal dish. Don't leave chopsticks crossed or standing upright in a bowl.

If you can't manage something with chopsticks, ask for a knife (*naifu*), fork (*foku*), or spoon (*supun*).

Never blow your nose in a restaurant. Find somewhere to hide first.

Pour drinks for your companions; leave it to them to pour yours. When they do, it's polite to hold your glass up to be filled.

65

SUSHI & SASHIMI

Not exactly raw fish

Among Westerners, plenty of fallacies exist on the subject of sushi and sashimi. "It's raw fish, right?" Not exactly. Morsels of raw fish, shellfish, and roes, as well as a few cooked varieties, pressed on to a pad of warm, vinegared rice—that's sushi (or more precisely, *nigirizushi*). Pieces of fish and vegetable rolled in rice and seaweed are *makizushi*. Delicate slices of raw fish and shellfish served with *daikon* (shredded white radish), *wasabi* (green horseradish paste), and soy sauce—that's sashimi, often served as a first course. Sushi can cost from ¥320 a selection to ¥2,400 (and even much more). If prices are not listed, ask—or you may face a shock when you receive the bill. The majority of sushi restaurants serve alchohol.

EDOGIN ($$)

Well established and popular, offering large servings of sashimi and made from the freshest fish from the famous market nearby. Until just before they're served, the fish are still swimming in a large tank in the center of the room. Reasonable prices.

✚ K7 ✉ 4-5-1 Tsukiji, Chuo-ku ☎ 3543–4401 🕐 Mon–Sat 11–9:30; Sun and hols 11:30–9 🚇 Tsukiji

FUKUSUKE ($)

This inexpensive sushi bar, popular with office workers, offers set meals, as well as sushi à la carte.

✚ K6 ✉ Toshiba Building B2, 5-2-1 Sotobori, Chuo-ku ☎ 3573–0471 🕐 Mon–Sat 11–10; Sun and hols 11:30–9 🚇 Ginza or Hibiya

FUKUZUSHI ($$$)

Not your usual sushi bar. A chic setting for great sushi in one of the liveliest nighttime areas downtown. Unlike most sushi restaurants, this one has a cocktail bar.

✚ G7 ✉ 5-7-8 Roppongi, Minato-ku ☎ 3402–4116 🕐 Mon–Sat 11:30–2, 5:30–11 🚇 Roppongi

GANKO ($$)

The sushi and sahimi ingredients here come from all over Japan and are always fresh. You can order in English.

✚ K6 ✉ 4-4-1 Ginza, Chuo-ku ☎ 3564–5678 🕐 Mon–Fri 11:30–11; Sat, Sun 11:30–10 🚇 Yurakucho JR

HEIROKUZUSHI ($)

A fast-service sushi bar where food is set out on a conveyor belt in front of the counter. Help youself to your favorites and pay at the end.

✚ E7 ✉ 5-8-5 Omotesando, Jingumae ☎ 3498–3968 🕐 Daily 11–9 🚇 Meijijingu-mae

KAKIYA SUSHI ($)

This stylish restaurant serves sushi.

✚ E7 ✉ 1-14-27 Jingumae, Shibuya-ku ☎ 3423–1400 🕐 Daily 11–11 🚇 Higashi-Ginza

KYUBEI ($$$)

Founded many years ago, and still going strong, Kyubei specializes in some of the most expertly made sushi around.

✚ K7 ✉ 8-7-6 Ginza, Chuo-ku ☎ 3571–6523 🕐 Mon–Sat 11:30–2, 5–10 🚇 Higashi-Ginza

RYU SUSHI ($$)

Little sushi bar next to the market halls; the owner is not the senior chef but another sort of artist, the painter Ryutaro Shiina.

✚ K7 ✉ 5-2-1 Tsukiji, Chuo-ku ☎ 3541–9517 🕐 Market days only Mon–Sat 7AM–2PM. Closed national and market holidays 🚇 Tsukiji

SUSHI DAI ($)

Try the *seto*, a set sushi course with tuna, eel, shrimp, and other morsels, plus rolls of tuna and rice in seaweed.

✚ L7 ✉ Tsukiji Fish Market, Tsukiji ☎ 3542–1111 🕐 Mon–Sat 5AM–2PM 🚇 Tsukiji

ITALIAN

CAPRICCIOSA ($)

A cheerful place that serves large portions of pasta and other Mediterranean favorties at fair prices. One of a chain with several branches.

➕ G7 ✉ 7-13-2 Roppongi, Minato-ku ☎ 5410–6061 🕒 Daily 11–11 Ⓜ Roppongi

CARMINE ($)

A small, friendly establishment with carefully prepared Tuscan-style antipasto, penne, and house specialties. Reservations are essential.

➕ G3 ✉ 21 Nakamachi, Shinjuku-ku ☎ 3260–5066 🕒 Mon–Sat noon–2, 6–9 Ⓜ Kagurazaka

CARMINE EDOCHIANO ($$)

Tuscan cuisine in a genteel old Japanese house. The setting alone makes it worth a visit.

➕ F5 ✉ 9-13 Arakicho, Shinjuku-ku ☎ 3225–6767 🕒 Daily 11:30–2, 6–9:30 Ⓜ Yotsuya-sanchome

IL BOCCALONE ($$$)

A north Italian-style trattoria, with good antipasti and grills and notable desserts.

➕ E9 ✉ 1-15-9 Ebisu, Shibuya-ku ☎ 3449–1430 🕒 Daily 11:30–2:30, 5–11 Ⓜ Ebisu

LA BOHÈME ($$)

Various pastas and sauces, pizzas, salads, and ice-creams. Popular with night owls.

➕ E7 ✉ Jubilee Plaza B1F, 5-8-5 Jingumae, Shibuya-ku ☎ 5467–5666 🕒 Daily 11:30AM– 4AM Ⓜ Omotesando

LA RANARITA AZUMBASHI ($$)

On the top floor of the Philippe Starck-desgined building, this restaurant offers both delicious pizzas and pasta and stunning views of Asakusa.

➕ N2 ✉ Asahi Beer Tower, 22nd floor, 1-23-1 Azumabashi, Asakusa ☎ 5608–5277 🕒 Mon–Sat 11:30–2. 5–9; Sun and hols 11.20–2, 4–8 Ⓜ Akasaka

LA VERDE ($)

Part of a chain, all of which are noted for their large servings of pasta with tasty toppings at low prices. The wines are also good and not expensive.

➕ F6 ✉ Aoyama Building B1F, 1-2-3 Kita-Aoyama, Minato-ku ☎ 3404–0712 🕒 Daily 11:30–2:30, 5:30–11 Ⓜ Aoyama-itchome

PENDIO ROSSO ($$)

Fresh, colorful salads, seafood, and steaks. In the same building as the Suntory Museum (► 53).

➕ G6 ✉ Tokyo Suntory Building 1F, 1-2-3 Moto-Akasaka 1F, Minato-ku ☎ 3470–1101 🕒 Daily 11:30–2, 5–11 Ⓜ Akasaka-mitsuke

ROSSO E NERO ($$)

Home cooking, with good antipasti, a wide choice of pastas, sauces, and grills. The menu includes Austrian as well as Italian dishes, notably the fruit strudel and dumpling desserts.

➕ G5 ✉ Kioi-cho Building 2F, 3-12 Kioi-cho, Chiyoda-ku ☎ 3237–5888 🕒 Daily 11:30–2, 5:30–11 Ⓜ Nagatacho

Prices

The prices given for non-Japanese restaurants (► 67–71) are for an average meal (starter and main course, or main course and dessert) per head, including service but excluding drinks.

$ up to ¥3,000

$$ ¥3,000–¥8,000

$$$ over ¥8,000

Lintaro ($$)

Lintaro Mizuhama is the friendly owner of the restaurant that bears his name, and he is often to be found chatting with diners or directing the service. He's a Ginza native and expert: his family has been here for centuries. The deep basement room is a surprise, with its high ceiling and Renaissance pictures. The food is Italian but Japanese notes in its presentation and flavors.The superbly fresh salads and vegetables are from the restaurant's special gardens.

➕ K7 ✉ 5-9-15 Ginza, Chuo-ku ☎ 3571–2037 🕒 Daily 11–2:30, 5–11. Closed New Year holiday Ⓜ Ginza

INDIAN & SRI LANKAN

Tomoca ($$)

This is an agreeable, relaxed Sri Lankan restaurant where you select your curry, choosing from shrimp, fish, chicken, or beef, and specify the degree of spiciness. (Don't ask for the hottest unless your digestive tract is made from Teflon.) A whole range of extras comes with it: poppadums, salads, fried eggplant, dal, and tangy *sambals*.

✚ E4 ✉ 1-7-27 Yotsuya, Shinjuku-ku ☎ 3353–7945 🕐 Daily 11–10:30 🚇 Shinjukugyoen-mae

AJANTA KOJIMACHI ($)

An old favorite, with the simplest of settings but one of the most comprehensive menus in Tokyo. The southern and northern Indian dishes are as authentic as you will find.

✚ G5 ✉ 3-11 Nibancho, Chiyoda-ku ☎ 3264–6955 🕐 Daily 24 hours 🚇 Kojimachi

ASHOKA ($$)

In a rather luxurious setting overlooking Chuo-dori, Ginza's main street, Ashoka serves curries and tasty tandoori-cooked chicken. Freshly made yogurt desserts are a specialty.

✚ K7 ✉ Pearl Building 2F, 7-9-18 Ginza, Chuo-ku ☎ 3572–2377 🕐 Mon–Sat 11:30–9:30; Sun 12–8:30 🚇 Higashi-Ginza

CEYLON INN ($)

The tables occupy several connecting rooms in an old house, with Sri Lankan folk-art, colorful curries and *sambals*, salads, and fruits.

✚ D10 ✉ 2-7-8 Kami-Meguro, Meguro-ku ☎ 3716–0440 🕐 Daily 11–2:30, 5–11 🚇 Nakameguro

KENBOKKE ($)

The decor here is modern with few Indian touches, but cuisine of the Bombay-born chef is authentic. Tandoori shrimp and chicken are specialties.

✚ F8 ✉ Empire Building 2F, 4-1-28 Nishi-Azabu, Minato-ku ☎ 3498–7080 🕐 Daily 11:30–11 🚇 Hiroo

MOTI ($)

An old favorite of locals and expatriates alike. Standard Indian interior and menu, with tasty vegetarian dishes, *kormas*, and chicken *masala*. One of five branches (others include Roppongi).

✚ H7 ✉ Kinpa Building 3F, 2-14-31 Akasaka, Minato-ku ☎ 3584–6640 🕐 Mon–Sat 11:30–11; Sun 12–10 🚇 Akasaka

PALETTE ($)

A plain café where Sri Lankan chefs make the curries as hot as you choose, or as mild. Breads and desserts are excellent.

✚ E9 ✉ 1-15-2 Ebisu-Nishi, Shibuya-ku ☎ 5489–0770 🕐 Daily 11:30–10:30 🚇 Ebisu

SAMRAT ($)

One of the first of the Indian wave and still popular, serving tandoori dishes and curries on the milder side. The Shibuya branch is open all night.

✚ G7 ✉ Shojikiya Building 3F, 4-10-10 Roppongi, Minato-ku ☎ 3478-5877 🕐 Daily 5–10 🚇 Roppongi
Also at:
✚ D8 ✉ Kiraku Building B1, 2-9-2 Udagawacho, Shibuya-ku ☎ 3370–7275 🕐 Daily 11–5AM 🚇 Shibuya

TANDOOR ($)

Good range of spicy meat and vegetarian curries in basic surroundings with friendly service.

✚ E9 ✉ 1-9-3 Ebisu-Nishi, Shibuya-ku ☎ 3461–6181 🕐 Daily 11–3, 6–11 🚇 Ebisu

THAI

BAN-THAI ($)

One of the city's oldest Thai restaurants, with a huge selection of dishes including delicious spicy warm salads. The curries are especially good.

✠ D4 ✉ 1-23-14 Kabuki-cho, East Shinjuku ☎ 3207–0068 🕐 Mon–Fri 11:30–3, 5–11; Sat, Sun and hols 11:30–11 🚇 Shinjuku

BENJARONG ($$)

An elegant restaurant, with cuisine to match, beautifully prepared by the former chef of a top Bangkok hotel. The menu is in English. Prices are lower at lunch than at dinner.

✠ D4 ✉ Miyata Building 2F, 1-4-12 Kabukicho, Shinjuku-ku ☎ 3209–7064 🕐 Mon–Sat 11:30–2, 5:30–10:30 🚇 Shinjuku

CAY ($$)

The Japanese-style Thai food at this trendy restaurant includes curries, salads, fried meats, and noodles. Live music some nights.

✠ E7 ✉ Spiral Building 5-6-123 Minami-Aoyama, Omotesando ☎ 3498–5790 🕐 Mon–Sat 5:30–11 🚇 Omotesando

CHIANG MAI ($$)

Customers are crammed into two small rooms to savor the standard dishes, cooked by two Thai chefs. Try the *tom yam gung* shrimp soup, the tangy fresh salads, and the spicy chicken.

✠ K6 ✉ 1-6-10 Yurakuchok, Chiyoda-ku ☎ 3580–0456 🕐 Daily 11–11 🚇 Hibiya

MAI-THAI ($$)

This is a small, cheerful, popular spot in a side street, serving a typical Thai menu at reasonable prices. One of a growing number of eating places in the fast-developing Ebisu.

✠ E9 ✉ 1-18-16 Ebisu, Shibuya-ku ☎ 3280–1155 🕐 Daily 11:30–2:30, 5–11 🚇 Ebisu

RICE TERRACE ($$)

A relaxed setting for some of Tokyo's best Thai food. Service is friendly but polished. Try to get a table downstairs: the upper level is cramped.

✠ F8 ✉ 2-7-9 Nishi-Azabu, Minato-ku ☎ 3498–6271 🕐 Daily 11:30–2, 5:30–11 🚇 Nogizaka

SIAM ($$)

A cut above the rest in Shinjuku's Kabukicho district, this restaurant specializes in northern Thai cooking. Intriguing spice combinations make the long menu, explained in English, quite an adventure.

✠ D4 ✉ Umemura Building 2F, 1-3-11 Kabukicho, Shinjuku-ku ☎ 3232–6300 🕐 Daily 5PM–3AM 🚇 Shinjuku

THE SIAM ($)

This one has been around for years and is still serving tasty Thai standards at prices that are economical—for Ginza—especially at lunchtime.

✠ K7 ✉ World Town Building 8F, 5-8-17 Ginza, Chuo-ku ☎ 3572–4101 🕐 Daily 11:30–2, 5:30–11 🚇 Higashi-Ginza

Chiang-Plai ($$)

Easily reached by the Hibya Line from Ginza, and just a short walk up the hill from the west exit of Ebisu Station, Chiang-Plai is a Bangkok-style café that features a large menu of tasty street-stand style fare. The adventurous chef is creative with his special dishes. The atmosphere is casual and friendly and prices are very reasonble.

✠ E9 ✉ 1-14-15 Ebisu-Minami, Ebisu ☎ 3715–4588 🕐 Daily 5–10:30PM 🚇 Ebisu

OTHER INTERNATIONAL FARE

Fusion Food

Californian and Australian chefs devised Pacific Rim cuisine by adding Asian ingredients to traditional European preparations. A similar process in reverse has produced a crop of restaurants in Tokyo where the dishes are western with a local twist, including Hiroyuki Masud's Bistro de Maido ($$), an informal restaurant in a Shibuyu basement that's popular with young business people. Salads topped with lightly salted seafoods are a specialty.

⊞ D7 ⊠ Miyagi Building B1, 1-10-12 Shibuya, Shibuyu-ku ☎ 3407–5724 ⏱ Daily 5:30–11:30PM. Closed Dec 31–Jan 4 🚇 Shibuya

ASENA ($$)
Authentic Turkish *meze* (hors d'oeuvres), kebabs, and much more, with a belly-dance show every Friday and Saturday.
⊞ H6 ⊠ Gojuban Building B1, 5-5-11 Akasaka, Minato-ku ☎ 3505–5282 ⏱ Daily 5–11 🚇 Akasaka

BENGAWAN SOLO ($$)
Indonesian furnishings, staff, and cooking. The colorful rijsttafel, including some highly spiced items, gives you a chance to experience the widest variety.
⊞ G7 ⊠ Kanako Building 1F, 7-18-13 Roppongi, Minato-ku ☎ 3408–5698 ⏱ Mon–Sat 11:30–2:30, 5–10 🚇 Roppongi

BOUGAINVILLEA ($$)
Vietnamese food may yet challenge Thai in Tokyo. This place has a wide choice of authentic dishes, including noodle soups, crab with coriander, spring rolls, sweet-and-sour pork or chicken, and meatballs.
⊞ D8 ⊠ Romanee Building 2F, 2-25-9 Dogenzaka, Shibuya-ku ☎ 3496–5537 ⏱ Daily 11:30–2, 5–11 🚇 Shibuya

CLUB KREISEL ($$)
German wurst, sauerkraut, beer, *sekt*, potatoes and wienerschnitzel, and the delicious red-fruit dessert called *rote grütze*.
⊞ G6 ⊠ OAG Haus 1F, 7-5-56 Akasaka, Minato-ku ☎ 3583–9488 ⏱ Daily 5–11 🚇 Akasaka

EL CASTELLANO ($$)
An informal and high-spirited Spanish establishment with a variety of tapas, tortillas, and wonderful paella. One of the only restaurants in Japan to serve rabbit.
⊞ E7 ⊠ 2-9-12 Shibuya, Omotesando ☎ 3407–7197 ⏱ Mon–Sat 6–11 🚇 Shibuya

MOMINOKI HOUSE ($)
A unique restaurant with a large contemporary Japanese–French menu. Live music on Saturday nights.
⊞ E7 ⊠ 2-18-5 Jingumae, Harajuku North ☎ 3405–9144 ⏱ Mon–Sat 11–10 🚇 Meijijingu-mae

ROSITA ($)
Guacamole, tacos, enchiladas, chili con carne, and other Mexican basics. Folksy.
⊞ D4 ⊠ Pegas-Kan Building B1, 3-31-5 Shinjuku, Shinjuku-ku ☎ 3356–7538 ⏱ Mon–Sat 11:30–2:30, 5:30–11 🚇 Shinjuku-san-chome

SAMOVAR ($$)
Authentic Russian stews and soups, kebabs, rye bread, beers, and vodkas.
⊞ D8 ⊠ 2-22-5 Dogenzaka, Shibuya-ku ☎ 3462–0648 ⏱ Mon–Sat 5–11 🚇 Shibuya

TOKAI-EN ($)
An enormous Korean operation, with all-you-can-eat bargain lunches. Spicy seafood, stews, and *bulgogi* barbecues are specialties. It can get boisterous in late evening.
⊞ D4 ⊠ 1-6-3 Kabukicho, Shinjuku-ku ☎ 3200–2934 ⏱ Daily 11AM–4AM 🚇 Shinjuku

BURGERS, DINERS & DELIS

ANDERSON ($)
A self-serve deli and sandwich bar located in the basement of a bakery.
✚ E7 ✉ 5-1-26 Aoyama, Minami-Aoyama
☎ 3407—4833 🕐 Mon—Fri 8AM—10PM; Sat, Sun 9AM—10PM
🚇 Omotesando

DOLE FRUIT CAFÉ ($)
Fresh fruits and vegetables come as juices, and in tasty combinations in curries and pizzas. Many vegetarian dishes.
✚ D8 ✉ Kokusai Building A-Kan 2F, 13-16 Udagawa-cho, Shibuya-ku ☎ 3464—6030
🕐 Daily 11—10 🚇 Shibuya

FARM GRILL ($)
A big, friendly place serving modern American salads, steaks, chili, pastas, and *teriyaki* chicken, plus reasonably priced drinks. On Sunday there's an all-you-can-eat and all-you-can-drink buffet.
✚ K6 ✉ Ginza Nine Sangokan Building 2F, 1-8-5 Ginza, Chuo-ku ☎ 5568—6156 🕐 Daily 11:30—2:30, 5—11
🚇 Ginza-itchome

GIRAFFE ($)
This cheerful café serves beer and a short menu of fast food and snacks, Japanese style.
✚ D8 ✉ BIR Building 1F, 32-15 Udagawa-cho, Shibuya-ku ☎ 3770—5577 🕐 Daily 11—11
🚇 Shibuya

GOOD HONEST GRUB ($)
A friendly place for brunch. Fresh fruit and vegetable juices plus vegetarian dishes.
✚ E9 ✉ 1-11-11 Ebisu-Minami, Shibuya-ku ☎ 3710—0400 🕐 Mon—Fri

11:30—11; Sat, Sun, national holidays 8:30—4:30PM, dinner until 11PM 🚇 Ebisu

HARVESTER ($)
KFC's chicken meals plus curries, sandwiches, and desserts.
✚ D7 ✉ 1-13-13 Omotesando, Jingumae
☎ 5411—7621 🕐 Daily 8AM —10:30PM 🚇 Harajuku JR

HOMEWORKS ($)
Above-average hamburgers with all the extras, plus salads, snacks, and sandwiches at above fast-food prices.
✚ F9 ✉ Shichiseisha Building 1F, 5-1-20 Hiroo, Shibuya-ku ☎ 3444—4560 🕐 Mon—Sat 11—9; Sun and holidays 11—6
🚇 Hiroo

JOHNNY ROCKETS ($)
Good hamburgers, french fries, salads, and other fast-food staples.
✚ G7 ✉ Coco Roppongi Building 2F, 3-11-10 Roppongi, Minato-ku ☎ 3423—1955
🕐 Sun—Thu 11—11; Fri, Sat 11AM—6AM 🚇 Roppongi

KUA'AINA ($)
Well-known for its huge Hawaiian hamburgers and sandwiches.
✚ E7 ✉ 5-10-21 Minami-Aoyama, Minato-ku
☎ 3407—8001 🕐 Mon—Sat 11AM—11:30PM; Sun and hols 11—10:30 🚇 Omotesando

NEWS DELI ($)
New York-inspired deli fare—salads, soups, sandwiches, pastas, and grills. Counter and tables, and take-out service.
✚ E7 ✉ SJ Building 1F, 3-6-23 Kita-Aoyama, Minato-ku
☎ 3407—1715 🕐 Daily 11—11
🚇 Omotesando

Sounds familiar
The Japanese have adapted the words as theye've adopted the food:

hot dog: *hotto doggu*

hamburger: *hambaga*

sandwich: *sando-ichi*

steak: *suteki*

ham: *hamu*

sausage: *soseji*

salad: *sarada*

bread: *pan*

butter: *bata*

coffee: *kohi*

bacon and egg: *bekon eggu*

orange juice: *orenji jusu*

ice cream: *aisu kurimu*

chocolate cake: *chokoreto keiki*

SHOPPING DISTRICTS

Price of paradise

The shops are a pleasure to visit, the range and quality of goods outstanding, the displays beautiful, the service usually impeccable. The customer is always right. Your most mundane purchase will be wrapped as though it were a jewel beyond price. Inflation has been low for decades and, with most foreign currencies increasing in value compared with the yen in recent years, prices are much more reasonable than they used to be.

Shopping is almost a national mania. It took only a few decades of prosperity to turn a frugal people into addicts of conspicuous consumption. Many stores open every day, typical hours being 10–6 or 10–8. There's always some sort of promotion; the marketing wizards never let up. Any excuse will do for a sales push, especially a holiday or festival. Purchases over ¥22,000 for export will be free of sales tax (carry your passport). In stores that don't expect foreigners, prices may be written in unfamiliar characters. Just ask: *Ikura desu-ka?* ("How much?")

AKIHABARA

For electrical and electronic equipment. At the JR station, look for signs to Electric Town, on the west side, where seven- and eight-floor buildings are stuffed with appliances piled in apparent confusion.
➕ L3 🚇 Akihabara
🚉 Akihabara

ASAKUSA

Nakamise-dori, near the temple, is a street of traditional little shops of all kinds.
➕ N2 🚇 Asakusa

GINZA-YURAKUCHO

For the famous department stores on Chuo-dori and in Yurakucho, and specialist shops, craft shops, and antiques shops, from Ginza 4-chome through 7-chome.
➕ K6–K7 🚇 Ginza, Higashi-Ginza 🚉 Yurakucho

JINGUMAE-HARAJUKU

Takeshita-dori for youth fashions and fads; Omotesando-dori for higher fashion and higher prices.
➕ E7 🚇 Meijijingu-mae, Omotesando 🚉 Harajuku

KANDA-JINBOCHO

An area with many secondhand bookstores stocking Japanese and foreign books and woodblock prints.
➕ J4 🚇 Jinbocho

MINAMI-AOYAMA

Antiques shops along and around Kotto-dori; fashion stores on Aoyama-dori and Omotesando-dori.
➕ F6–F7 🚇 Omotesando

SHIBUYA

For department stores, fashion boutiques, bookstores, and home improvement stores.
➕ D8 🚇 🚉 Shibuya

SHINJUKU

Camera and audio-visual equipment stores west and east of the station; department stores above and east of the station.
➕ D4–E4 🚉 Shinjuku 🚇 Shinjuku, Shinjuku-sanchome

UENO

The Ameyoko market (short for Ameya Yokocho) is packed with stands selling food, household goods, and clothes, under the elevated tracks from Ueno to Okachimachi JR Station. "Motorcycle heaven," rows of show-rooms, shiny machines, accessories and parts, is northeast of Ueno JR Station along Showa-dori.
➕ L2 🚇 Ueno, Ueno-Hirokoji

DEPARTMENT STORES

The *depato* is a Japanese institution. Visit at least one of the big ones to experience the phenomenon. The layout of the stores is easy to understand, they take credit cards, they can produce someone who speaks English, they stock almost everything, they are close to stations (they may own a line or two), and they open on weekends—big days for shopping. Closing day varies from store to store.

ISETAN

An enormous store above Shinjuku-sanchome station, with dozens of designer boutiques. The food hall and restaurants are in the basement. Good deals for visitors.

➕ D4 ✉ 3-14-1 Shinjuku, Shinjuku-ku ☎ 3352–1111
🕐 Thu—Tue 10–7 🚇 Shinjuku
🚇 Shinjuku-sanchome

MATSUYA

Bright, colorful and favored by younger customers. The basement food hall sells excellent box meals at sensible prices.

➕ K6 ✉ 3-6-1 Ginza, Chuo-ku ☎ 3567–1211
🕐 Mon—Wed, Fri 10–6; Sat, Sun and national holidays 10–6:30
🚇 Ginza

MITSUKOSHI

Founded in the 17th century, with selections of toys, stationery, kimonos, and sportswear, and a fine food hall.

➕ L5 ✉ 1-4-1 Nihonbashi-Muromachi, Chuo-ku ☎ 3241–3311 🕐 Tue—Sat 10–6; Sun and holidays 10–6:30
🚇 Mitsukoshi-mae

ODAKYU

Above part of Shinjuku Station, with its own railroad line. Food is in the lower basement, the 12th floor has an art gallery, and restaurants are on the 15th floor and top floor.

➕ D4 ✉ 1-1-3 Nishi-Shinjuku, Shinjuku-ku ☎ 3342–1111
🕐 Wed—Mon 10–7
🚇 Shinjuku

SEIBU

With adjoining Parco fashion store and theater complex. Designer boutiques, children's wear, stationery. Top-floor restaurants. Other branches in Ikebukuro and Yurakucho.

➕ D8 ✉ 21-1 Udagawa-cho, Shibuya-ku ☎ 3462–0111
🕐 Thu—Tue 10–8:30
🚇 Shibuya

TAKASHIMAYA

The basement food hall has Fauchon and Fortnum & Mason counters. Elegant displays, immaculately turned-out staff and boutiques with famous-name fashions.

➕ L5 ✉ 2-4-1 Nihonbashi, Chuo-ku ☎ 3211–4111
🕐 Thu—Tue 10–7
🚇 Nihonbashi
Also at:
➕ D4 ✉ Times Square (south of the station) 🚇 Shinjuku

TOKYU

The latest fashions for its mostly younger customers. The basement food hall is up there with the best

➕ D8 ✉ 2-24 Dogenzaka, Shibuya ☎ 3477–3111
🕐 Daily 10–8 🚇 Shibuya

In-store food

Department stores are a boon to visitors, and not only when they want to shop or to use the restroom facilities. Most stores have a whole selection of reasonably priced restaurants offering different food styles, normally on the top floor. But in the basement, their food-to-go departments are an eye-opener, and an education in the ingredients of Japanese cuisine. The artistically prepared box lunches are a comparative bargain, and—if your budget is really restricted—you can taste all sorts of free samples, although they are more likely to sharpen your appetite than satisfy it.

CRAFTS & SOUVENIRS

Everyday quality

If the price of fine porcelain and lacquerware comes as a shock, look instead at the everyday versions sold in street markets and department stores. The Japanese sense of color and form extends to these too, and quality is usually faultless. Even the disposable baskets and boxes used for take-out meals can be minor craftworks. Special handmade and decorative papers, in the form of wrappings, stationery, boxes, dolls, fans, and origami designs make good gifts—light, unbreakable and reasonably priced.

CRAFTS

BINGO-YA

Folk art, crafts, traditional toys, and gifts from all parts of Japan.
F3 ✉ 10-6 Wakamatsu-cho, Shinjuku-ku
☎ 3202–8778 ◷ Thu–Sun 10–7 Ⓜ Akebonobashi (15-minute walk)

INTERNATIONAL ARCADE

Thirty shops selling crafts and souvenirs, from the superb to the frankly junky. Several pearl shops.
J6 ✉ 1-7-23 Uchisaiwaicho, Chiyoda-ku
◷ Daily 10–6 Ⓜ Hibiya

ORIENTAL BAZAAR

Four levels of handicrafts, souvenirs, antiques, bric-à-brac, dolls, and kimonos. Omotesando-dori
H3, M13 ✉ 5-9-13 Jingumae, Shibuya-ku
☎ 3400–3933 ◷ Fri–Wed 9:30–6:30 Ⓜ Omotesando

DOLLS

KYUGETSU

An established shop, selling traditional and many other dolls, in wood, papier mâché, and fabric.
M4 ✉ 1-20-4 Yanagibashi, Taito-ku ☎ 3861–5511
◷ Daily 9:15–6 Ⓜ Asakusabashi

CERAMICS

KISSO

Fine ceramics combine traditional methods with modern designs. Shares premises with a restaurant.
G7 ✉ Axis Building B1F, 5-17-1, Roppongi, Minato-ku
☎ 3582–4191 ◷ Daily 11:30–2, 5:30–9 Ⓜ Roppongi

KORANSHA

Fine pieces, especially the flower and bird patterns from Arita in Kyushu.
K7 ✉ 5-12-12 Ginza, Chuo-ku ☎ 3543–0951
◷ Mon–Sat 9:30–6:30
Ⓜ Higashi-Ginza

PAPER ART

KYUKYODO

Beautiful handmade papers and everything needed for calligraphy.
K7 ✉ 5-7-4 Ginza, Chuo-ku ☎ 3571–4429
◷ Daily 10–6 Ⓜ Ginza

WASHIKOBO

Washi and *mingei* (folkcraft) items.
G7 ✉ 1-8-10 Nishi-Azabu, Minato-ku ☎ 3405-1841
◷ Mon–Sat 10–6 Ⓜ Roppongi

ORIGAMI KAIKAN
(► 61)

FOR CHILDREN

KIDDYLAND

Sells the toys, alarm clocks, and kitsch that childhood dreams are made of.
E7 ✉ 6-1-9 Jingumae, Shibuya-ku ☎ 3409–3431
◷ Daily 10–8 Ⓜ Harajuku
Ⓜ Meijijingu-mae

POKEMON MUSEUM

The Pocket Monsters game and cartoon series have spun off a whole world of little creatures, and all are available here.
L5 ✉ Kawasaki Teitoku Building 1F, 3-2-5 Nihonbashi, Chuo-ku ☎ 5200–0707
◷ Daily 11–8 Ⓜ Nihonbashi

ANTIQUES, ORNAMENTS & JUNK

FUJI-TORI
Established in 1948, this reputable dealer carries quality antiques and works of art.
🔲 E7 ✉ 6-1-10 Jingumae, Shibuya-ku ☎ 3400–2777 🕐 Wed–Mon 11:30–6 🚇 Meijijingu-mae

HASEBE-YA ANTIQUES
An eclectic stock of pottery, bronze statuary, *netsuke*, lacquerware, and woodware—boxes, carvings, and furniture.
🔲 G8 ✉ 1-5-24 Azabujuban, Minato-ku ☎ 3401–9998 🕐 Mon–Sat 10:30–6 🚇 Roppongi

KAMON ANTIQUES
For oriental fine art and folk art, calligraphy, and Imari ware.
🔲 E8 ✉ 4-3-12 Shibuya, Shibuya-ku ☎ 3406–1765 🕐 Mon–Sat 10:30–6 🚇 Shibuya

KUROFUNE ANTIQUES
A colorful shop, well-stocked with fine porcelain, old prints, lacquerware, furniture, and folk art.
🔲 G7 ✉ 7-7-4 Roppongi B1F, Minato-ku ☎ 3479–1552 🕐 Mon–Sat 10–6 🚇 Roppongi

FLEA MARKETS

Sales of used goods and junk were traditionally held outside the gates of temples and shrines, and some still are. There's a tradition of settling debts before the New Year, and some people find it necessary to sell their possessions. Harder times have now made it more respectable to buy secondhand goods. Real bargains are rare, and dealers will normally have latched on to them almost before the market opens. Even so, it pays to get to the sale early, as the dealers are laying out their wares. The sales are an unusual chance to bargain. Listings magazines (▶ 91) give details of upcoming sales. Regular sites and days include:

AOYAMA OVAL PLAZA
🔲 E7 ✉ Near National Children's Castle, Jingumae 5-chome, Shibuya-ku 🕐 Every 3rd Sat of month 6–sunset 🚇 Omotesando

HANAZONO SHRINE
🔲 E4 ✉ Opposite Marui Interior store, Shinjuku-sanchome 🕐 Every Sun 7–6 🚇 Shinjuku, Shinjuku-sanchome

NOGI SHRINE
🔲 G7 ✉ Roppongi, Minato-ku 🕐 Every 2nd Sun of month 7–6 🚇 Nogizaka

ROI BUILDING
🔲 G7 ✉ In front of Roi Building, Roppongi 5-chome, Minato-ku 🕐 Every 4th Thu and Fri of month 7–6 🚇 Roppongi

SALVATION ARMY BAZAAR
🔲 A4 ✉ 2-21-2 Wada, Suginami-ku 🕐 Every Sat 9–1 🚇 Nakano-Fujimicho (see map at station)

TOGO SHRINE
🔲 E7 ✉ Harajuku, Shibuya-ku 🕐 Every 1st, 4th and 5th Sun of month 4AM–2PM 🚇 Meijijingu-mae

Collectible "antiques"

Antiques (which in Japan are anything more than about 50 years old), are generally expensive. Fine pieces fetch enormous sums, although the market has settled down since the 1980s' boom. Specifically, Japanese collectibles include ceramics, dolls, swords, lacquerware, masks, *netsuke*—a small and often intricately carved toggle of ivory or wood, used to fasten a small container to a kimono sash—paintings, woodcarvings, and woodblock prints (▶ 53, panel). Before exploring, look at the shops in or near the big hotels to get an idea of what is available and how much it costs, although hotel prices are at the top of the range.

MISCELLANEOUS STORES

High fashion

The elegant young OL (➤ 7) in search of the latest designs patrols the fashion boutiques, conveniently clustered in "vertical malls." You can see her in action at:

La Forêt

✚ E7 ✉ 1-11-16 Jingumae, Shibuya-ku

🕐 Daily 10:30–7

🚇 Meijijingu-mae

From 1st Building

✚ F7 ✉ 5-3-10 Minami-Aoyama, Minato-ku 🕐 Daily 10:30–7 🚇 Omotesando

BOOKS

AOYAMA BOOK CENTER

Large stock of American and European titles.

✚ G7 ✉ 6-1-20 Roppongi, Minato-ku ☎ 3479–0479

🕐 Daily 10–5:30AM

🚇 Roppongi

Also at:

✚ F9 ✉ Hiroo Garden Plaza, 4-1-29 Minami-Azabu, Minato-ku

🚇 Hiroo

ISSEIDO

For secondhand and antique books, art books, and woodblock prints.

✚ J4 ✉ 1-7 Kanda-Jinbocho, Chiyoda-ku ☎ 3292–0071

🕐 Daily 10–7 🚇 Jinbocho

KINOKUNIYA

Close to the south exit of Shinjuku Station. The large stock of foreign books is on the 7th floor.

✚ D5 ✉ Annex Building, Times Square, 5-24-2 Sendagaya, Shibuya-ku ☎ 5361–3301

🕐 Daily 10–7 🚇 Shinjuku

Also at:

✚ D8 ✉ Tokyu Plaza, 1-2-2 Dogenzaka, Shibuya-ku

MARUZEN

Imported books, travel books, and others about every aspect of Japanese life. Good for woodblock prints.

✚ L5 ✉ 2-3-10 Nihonbashi, Chuo-dori ☎ 3272–7211

🕐 Mon–Sat 10–7

🚇 Nihonbashi.

Also at:

✚ D8 ✉ Bunkamura B1F, 2-24-1 Dogenzaka, Shibuya-ku

OHYA-SHOBO

Among several second-hand book and print shops clustered along the road heading east from the station, this one has a vast stock of antique illustrated books and fine prints.

✚ J4 ✉ 1-1 Kanda-Jinbocho, Chiyoda-ku ☎ 3291–0062

🕐 Daily 10–7 🚇 Jinbocho

HOBBIES

TOKYU HANDS

Everything you might need for model-making, sewing, painting, carpentry, and much more.

✚ D8 ✉ 12-18 Udagawa-cho, Shibuya-ku ☎ 5489–5111

🕐 Daily 10–7 🚇 Shibuya

Also at:

✚ D5 ✉ Times Square, near Shinjuku Station 🚇 Shinjuku

STATIONERY

ITO-YA

Stationery, wrapping paper, and greeting cards—Japanese and imported. Picture framing, art supplies, and ingenious desk accessories.

✚ K6 ✉ 2-7-15 Ginza, Chuo-ku ☎ 3561–8311 🕐 Daily 10:30–7 🚇 Ginza

PEARLS

MIKIMOTO

This is the big name, in the field of cultured pearls. Expect to pay top prices.

✚ K6 ✉ 4-5-5 Ginza, Chuo-ku ☎ 3535–4611 🕐 Thu–Tue 10–6 🚇 Ginza

TASAKI PEARL

This store has several showrooms, and offers tours and demonstrations. City tour buses often include a visit.

✚ H7 ✉ 1-3-3 Akasaka, Minato-ku ☎ 5561–8881

🕐 Daily 9–6 🚇 Akasaka

CAMERAS & ELECTRONICS

Don't expect any real bargains. Prices may be higher than in your home country, even for Japanese-made products, although this depends on exchange rates. But it is still fascinating to see the range on offer in Japan and the local marketing methods. Tell the sales staff where you are from, so that you get the right specification of equipment: Japanese electronic stores cater to all markets.

LAOX
This giant electrical retailer has four buildings in Akihabara—the main one looks like a huge VCR standing on end. The duty-free branch is nearby at 1-13-3 Soto-Kanda. Also toys and pearls.
⊕ L3 ✉ 1-2-9 Soto-Kanda, Chiyoda-ku ☎ 3253–7111
⏰ Mon–Sat 10–7:45; Sun 10–7:15 🚇 Akihabara

MINAMI
Five floors are packed with electrical equipment, a surprising seventh floor with imported furniture, including antiques.
⊕ L3 ✉ 4-3-3 Soto-Kanda, Chiyoda-ku ☎ 3255-8030
⏰ Daily 9–5:30 🚇 Akihabara

YAMAGIWA
This store, one of the biggest retailers in Akihabara, specializes in lighting fixtures and sells everything from light bulbs to satellite dishes, You'll find both domestic and imported lines.
⊕ L3 ✉ 4-1-1 Soto-Kanda, Chiyoda-ku ☎ 3253–2111
⏰ Sun–Thu 10–5:30; Fri–Sat 10–8 🚇 Akihabara

PHOTOGRAPHIC EQUIPMENT

New means expensive, but since the Japanese photographer must have the latest, there is a lot of secondhand gear available at more sensible prices.

SAKURAYA
Not only cameras and film, but video equipment and electronics galore.
⊕ D4 ✉ 2-29-11 Shinjuku, Shinjuku-ku ☎ 3352–4711
⏰ Daily 10–8 🚇 Shinjuku

YODOBASHI CAMERA
Near the west exit of Shinjuku Station. A glitzy, multi-level, noisy, crowded store full of every sort of equipment and film. There's a branch east of the station.
⊕ D4 ✉ 1-11-1 Nishi-Shinjuku, Shinjuku-ku ☎ 3346–1010 ⏰ Daily 9:30–9:30 🚇 Shinjuku

MUSIC TAPES & CDS

HMV
Tens of thousands of CDs, cassettes, and videos are in stock. The dozens of listening stations are often not enough for the crowds.
⊕ D8 ✉ 24-1 Udagawa-cho, Shibuya ☎ 5458–3411
⏰ Daily 10–10 🚇 Shibuya

TOWER RECORDS
One of the world's biggest retailers, with eight floors stocking every style of recorded music.
⊕ D7 ✉ 1-22-14 Jinnan, Shibuya-ku ☎ 3496-3661
⏰ Daily 10–10 🚇 Shibuya

Akihabara
Several blocks of multistory emporia are stuffed with everything from electronic marvels to workaday washing machines. Smaller stores specialize in computer software, mobile phones, speaker systems, and even humble switches and cables. Goods flow out on to the street; sound systems are playing at pain threshhold. A lot of signs are in Russian. Carry your passport to benefit from duty-free concessions, and ask for discounts on any pretext you can think of.

JAPANESE THEATER & ARTS

People's theater

Kabuki developed under the Tokugawa *shoguns*, and two prohibitions gave it the character is still has today. In 1629, women were banned from the stage, resulting in the tradition of *onnagata*—male actors specializing in female roles. Then it was forbidden to attend the plays wearing swords. The *samurai* class, who wouldn't be seen in public without a sword, stayed away, and *kabuki* became an entertainment for the masses. The plays blend historical romance, tragedy, and comedy, music, dance, and acrobatics, performed in vivid costumes and makeup.

KABUKI

The Kabuki-za Theater is a Ginza landmark, with its big hanging lanterns and posters. Full programs last four to five hours, including two intermissions; tickets cost upwards of ¥3,000 (¥13,000 for good seats). You can rent an English-language "Earphone Guide," synchronized to the action and an English program is invaluable. You can opt for a one-act play, up to an hour long, for about ¥1,000 for a non-reservable, distant fiifth-floor seat, but the earphone cannot be used on the the fifth floor.

KABUKI-ZA THEATER
🚇 K7 ✉ 4-12-15 Ginza, Chuo-ku ☎ 3541–3131 🚉 Higashi-Ginza

NATIONAL THEATER (KOKORITSU GEJIKO)
🚇 H5 ✉ 4-1 Hayabusa-cho, Chiyoda-ku ☎ 3265–7411 🚉 Hanzomon

NOH

Much older than *kabuki*, infinitely stylized, and performed by masked actors, *noh* is less accessible still to foreigners. Even the Japanese confess to wishing it didn't go on so long, and so slowly. The younger generation says "*Noh*? No!" Listings magazines (► 91) will tell you about the open-air, torch-lit performances at temples, where even the uninitiated can enjoy the gorgeous costumes and setting. A regular indoor venue is:

KANZE NOH-GAKUDO
🚇 D8 ✉ 1-16-4 Shoto, Shibuya-ku ☎ 3469–5241 🚉 Shibuya

BUNRAKU

In this form of theater, three puppeteers work near-lifesize figures, while narrators tell the stories to a musical accompaniment. Like *noh*, it is an esoteric art for which few foreigners acquire a taste. Performances are sometimes staged at the small hall of the National Theater (see above).

BONSAI

By carefully pruning roots and branches, a tree sapling can be kept to a miniature scale while reaching maturity. The aim is to produce a tree that looks natural in every way, except size. Some prized specimens, gnarled and apparently windswept, have been handed down for over 200 years. Check out:
Takagi Bonsai Museum
🚇 G4 ✉ 1-1 Goban-cho, Chiyoda-ku ☎ 3221–0006 🕐 Tue–Sun 10–7 🚉 Ichigaya JR

IKEBANA

The art of flower arranging developed in parallel with the tea ceremony to decorate the room in a simple but exquisite fashion. The Tourist Information Center (► 91) can tell you about classes.

MUSIC & MOVIES

CLASSICAL MUSIC

Japanese soloists and conductors have taken the world by storm, and standards of performance in Tokyo are excellent. Many foreign soloists, orchestras, and opera companies also appear. Ticket prices are high (¥3,000–¥25,000). Among the many concert halls are:

BUNKAMURA ORCHARD HALL

Part of an impressive cultural center, with a theater and movie theaters.
✚ D8 ✉ 2-24-1 Dogenzaka, Shibuya-ku ☎ 3477–9111 🚇 Shibuya

SUNTORY HALL

A fine new concert hall in the Ark Hills development.
✚ H7 ✉ 1-13-1 Akasaka, Minato-ku ☎ 3584–9999 🚇 Tameike-sanno

TOKYO METROPOLITAN FESTIVAL HALL

Located at the entrance to Ueno Park. Seats 2,300 in the main hall, 700 in a smaller auditorium. A small shop in the foyer sells sheet music and souvenirs.
✚ L2 ✉ 5-45 Ueno Koen, Taito-ku ☎ 3828–2111 🚇 Ueno

TOKYO OPERA CITY

Despite its name, this new theater and art gallery complex presents a varied orchestral concert program.
✚ C4 ✉ 3-20-2 Nishi-Shinjuku, Shinjuku-ku ☎ 5353–0770 🚇 Hatsudai

JAZZ

Many local and touring musicians appear in Roppongi and Harajuku clubs. Blue Note Tokyo seems to book the biggest visiting names, but ticket prices are expensive, starting at ¥8,000. Listings magazines tell who is in town (➤ 91).

BLUE NOTE TOKYO

✚ E7 ✉ 5-13-3 Minami-Aoyama, Minato-ku ☎ 3407–5781 🚇 Omotesando

POP & ROCK CONCERTS

Local and visiting stars perform at the Tokyo Dome (➤ 82), and on summer evenings outdoors in Hibiya Park (➤ 40). Another indoor venue is:

NIPPON BUDOKAN HALL

The martial arts arena built for the 1964 Olympics.
✚ J4 ✉ 2-3 Kitanomaru Koen, Chiyoda-ku ☎ 3216–5100 🚇 Kudanshita

MOVIES

Most movies come from Hollywood and are shown with the original soundtracks and Japanese subtitles. Smaller "boutique" theaters screen later performances and provide an infinitely varied diet, including classics, reruns, and European movies. Tickets are around ¥1,800. For a little more money, you can reserve seats. Check the listings in the local English-language publications (➤ 91).

Central ticket agencies

For most theaters, concert halls, and major sports arenas, you can reserve tickets up to the day before the performance at agencies such as:

Kyukyodo

✚ K7 ✉ 5-7-4 Ginza, Chuo-ku ☎ 3571–4429 🚇 Higashi-Ginza

Play Guide Honten

✚ K6 ✉ 2-6-4 Ginza, Chuo-ku ☎ 3561–8821 🚇 Ginza
On the day of the performance, telephone the venue and arrange to collect the tickets there; if you have a problem making yourself understood, ask someone at your hotel to make the call.

ENTERTAINMENT DISTRICTS

Meeting point

Everyone in Tokyo knows the statue of Hachiko, an Akita dog who used to walk with his master, a university professor, to Shibuya Station each morning, and meet him off the train again in the evening. One day in 1925, the professor did not return: he had suddenly been taken ill and died. Hachiko waited for the last train and then sadly made his way home. For seven years, he came every evening to wait, until at last he too died. Touched by such loyalty, the people of Tokyo paid for the bronze statue outside the station.

"Like calls to like" is the Japanese equivalent of "birds of a feather," and it certainly applies to Tokyo's nightspots. The crowds go where the action is, so ever more places open up in these areas in order to tap the market.

AKASAKA

Two parallel streets, Hitotsugi-dori and Tamachi-dori, and the narrow alleyways between them are packed with bars, clubs, and restaurants. It's respectable and rather expensive, although not quite in the Ginza league, and mostly frequented by company men on expense accounts and people staying at the area's big hotels.

GINZA

The prices in the clubs and top restaurants are legendary, and prohibitive for anyone not on an unlimited expense account. Others can enjoy the street scene, find a fast-food or budget restaurant, and enjoy a drink in one of the afford-able bars or big beer halls.

IKEBUKURO

The streets around Ikebukro Station, particularly the west side, have a vibrant nightlife and are popular with shoppers on the weekend. The crowds here are more diverse than, say, Ginza, and it is a great district to come face-to-face with a cross-section of Toyoites. It is one of the most densely populated areas of the city.

ROPPONGI

This is a favorite with Tokyo's younger foreign contingent as well as more adventurous Japanese, partly because it's still awake at 4AM, while elsewhere has quietened down by midnight. The Almond coffee house at the main street crossing near the subway station is a popular rendezvous and landmark. There's a huge choice of eating and drinking places nearby, but prices have risen in recent years to rival Akasaka levels. Drunks may be a problem in a few of the lower-priced bars and discos.

SHIBUYA

Busy and cheerful, with a mainly young crowd, this popular stopping and entertainment district is not as expensive as Akasaka. There's a host of fast-food outlets and a wide choice of ethnic restaurants. Local groups play in the live music bars.

SHINJUKU

As the gateway to the city from the west, Shinjuku has always entertained travelers. The railroad gave it a boost, and Kabukicho northeast of the station is Japan's biggest red-light district. From respectable bars and fine restaurants, the nightlife runs the range, testing the limits of legality. Women in vinyl miniskirts hand out addresses and prices of massage parlors; hard-faced barkers urge passers-by to see strip shows and bottomless bars.

OTHER IDEAS

A night out can be costly, unless you are being entertained by local business contacts, who will expect to pick up the bill (you can return the hospitality when they visit your home country). You are not likely to be invited to a Japanese home until you know someone very well; anyway, most people eat out more than they do at home.

LOCAL CHOICES

Robatayaki restaurants are cheerful, noisy places where varied foods are cooked on an open grill amid clouds of smoke. A *ryori-ya* or *shokudo* is a mixed-menu restaurant: plastic replicas in the window show the choices and prices. *Chuka ryori-ya* are basic Chinese restaurants serving such staples as fried rice and noodle dishes. *Ramen-ya* and *soba-ya* serve inexpensive bowls of noodles in a soup or with a topping. A *kissaten* is a coffee house serving light snacks and sweet pastries —the coffee may be expensive, but you can sit as long as you like. For a moderately priced breakfast of toast, coffee, a boiled egg, and small salad, ask for *moningu sabisu* ("morning service").

BARS

The variety is endless. Take a look inside and decide if the atmosphere appeals to you. If prices are not posted, ask for a list. Bottles of good French or Australian wine start from about ¥2,000. Beers run from ¥500 to ¥800 or more. The good, if rather bland, local whiskey costs much less than imported brands. Bars and clubs where local or Western groups perform ("live houses") generally make an extra charge of ¥1,000–1,500. A *nomi-ya* is an informal neighborhood bar, also known as *akachochin*, and indicated by the red lantern outside. *Karaoke* bars have spread round the world like wildfire, but this is where the idea of amateur singing to a tape was born. Unless you want to fork out a large fee (¥5,000 an hour is typical), avoid bars where a hostess sits with you while you have an outrageously expensive drink (in less legitimate places other services can be negotiated).

DISCOS

Most are in Shibuya, Shinjuku, and especially Roppongi, where the Square Building alone houses discos on most of its ten floors. It is impossible to predict from day to day which will be jumping and which empty or closed for good. Ask local contacts and check listings magazines (▶ 91). A cover charge about ¥4,000 includes a couple of drink tickets. The down-side of the disco scene is the growth of aggressive behavior, fueled by alcohol. When the atmosphere turns nasty, it is best to leave and find somewhere else.

Beer halls

These big, informal places, vaguely modeled on German *bierkeller*, are mostly run by the brewery companies. You sit at large or small tables, or bar counters, and order beers and plates of savory snacks—three or four add up to a meal. In addition, many department stores turn their roofs into beer gardens during the sultry summers. Top beer halls include:

Beer Station Sapporo
✚ E10 ✉ Yebisu Garden Place, 3 Ebisu, Shibuya-ku
🚇 Ebisu

Flamme d'Or Asahi
✚ Off map ✉ Asahi Brewery, 1 Azumabashi, Sumida-ku
🚇 Asakusa

Kirin City
✚ K6 ✉ Bunshodo Building 2F, 3-4-12 Ginza, Chuo-ku
🚇 Ginza

SPORTS & SPORTING VENUES

Big stars

For many years, few foreigners undertook the rigorous training, let alone reached the senior ranks of *sumo*. The picture changed in the late 1980s when a Hawaiian known as Konishiki became a frequent winner. Then came an Irish-Polynesian, Akebono, who became the sole *yokozuna* (grand champion). The Japanese tolerated the invasion, while hoping for a home-grown hero, so there was relief at the promotion of Takanohana to *yokozuna* rank in 1994. Television has made *sumo* stars into national figures. Most of the training stables are in Ryogoku, and some permit visitors to watch morning practice sessions between 5 and 10:30AM. Get a Japanese speaker to make an appointment for you.

Azumazeki Stable

☎ 3624–0033

Kazugano Stable

☎ 3631–1871

SUMO

Literally "fat power," this form of wrestling was originally practiced at Shinto shrines and is surrounded by time-honored ceremony. After purification and other rituals, the two huge contenders collide, each intent on unbalancing the other and tipping him over or forcing him from the ring. *Basho* tournaments take place in January, May, and September. Tickets for good seats are expensive, although they include a good box meal. Bouts are televised from 4 to 6PM each day of the tournament. The main Tokyo venue is:

KOKUGIKAN SUMO HALL

✚ N4 ✉ 1-3-28 Yokoami, Sumida-ku ☎ 3623–5111 🕓 10–6 (main bouts 3–6) 🚇 Ryogoku

BASEBALL

If there is a Japanese natural sport, this is it—top players and managers become media superstars. Tokyo has several teams in the two major leagues and one of them usually wins the Japan Series play-off. The season is from April to October, and the main venue is:

TOKYO DOME

This 55,000-seat capacity stadium is the where the baseball action is.

✚ J3 ✉ 1-3-61 Koraku, Bunkyo-ku ☎ 3811–2111 🚇 Suidobashi

GOLF

It seems as if half of Tokyo's businessmen claim to play, but the game is expensive and the courses remote. They console themselves at driving ranges, whose big net cages are a feature of the skyline.

TENNIS

Some big hotels have courts, even in Tokyo itself as do the Tokyo Bay resorts. Hibiya Park (► 40) in the city center has public courts.

SWIMMING

The nearest reasonably clean beach is at Enoshima near Kamakura (► 20), which is crowded, especially on weekends, from June to the end of August, and deserted the rest of the year. Toshima-en amusement park (► 62) has several swimming pools; Yoyogi Park's sports center has a large one, but it's often in use for events.

PLACES TO JOG

Traffic pollution and pavement congestion make the streets a less than enjoyable place to jog, but there's a park within easy reach of most hotels. Best of all is the Imperial Palace Garden (► 36). Shinjuku has its "Central Park" (► 28). Many big hotels provide jogging maps.

BATH HOUSES

The earth's crust seems especially thin in Japan. The unstable ground threatens disaster in the form of earthquakes and *tsunami* and creates countless hot springs. Tokyo is no exception. Coffee-colored, mineral-rich water from beneath the city is piped to dozens of *onsen* (hot spring-fed baths); other public baths are called *sento*. They traditionally served as community centers where local people gathered to relax, and in older parts of the city they still do. These days, the sexes are generally segregated: only in some open-air rural spas is there mixed bathing. Three traditional *onsen* in Tokyo are:

ASAKUSA KANNON ONSEN

A large and very hot bath esteemed for its curative properties.
🟥 N2 ✉ Asakusa 2-chome, Taito-ku ☎ 3844–4141
🕐 Daily 6:30AM–6:30PM
🚇 Asakusa

AZABU JUBAN KASHINOYU

A cozy *onsen*, in an unlikely location, the third floor of a modern building.
🟥 G8 ✉ 1-5-22 Azabu Juban, Minato-ku ☎ 3401–8324
🕐 Wed–Mon 3–11
🚇 Roppongi

HOTEL SUEHIRO

Very hot natural spring bath with sauna and steam room.
🟥 Off map to west
✉ 8-1-5 Nishikamata, Otaku
☎ 3734–6561 🕐 Daily 6AM–9AM , 1–midnight
🚇 Kamata

ORDER OF THE BATH

• On entering, take off all your clothes in the locker room.
• Take only your towel, soap, and shampoo into the bath room.
• Sit on one of the stools away from the bath.
• Douse yourself with water using a scoop, bucket, or shower, whatever is provided.
• Wash thoroughly all over and meticulously rinse off all the soap. *No trace of soap must get into the bath itself.*
• Immerse yourself gradually in the bath (*ofuro*). If there's a choice, try the less hot bath first. Temperatures typically range from 108°F up to about 118°F.
• Don't put your head underwater.
• If you feel dizzy, get out.
• Some users recommend getting in and out several times.
• Don't drink alcohol before the bath.

If you're staying in a private house, much the same rules apply. Replace the cover on the bath to keep the water hot for other users. In a *ryokan* (▶ 86), which may have a bath for couples or families as well as the men's and women's, the maid will usually ask you when you would like to take your bath, and come to let you know when it is ready. The accepted bath time in a *ryokan* or private home is before the evening meal.

Ritual

Tthe Shinto code emphasizes purity and cleanliness, not only of the mind but of the body. Faith and medical research agree that a hot, deep bath is beneficial to health, reducing stress and tension and relieving aches and pains.

"Soaplando" massage parlors are less concerned with the spiritual element—the masseuses coat their own bodies and the client's with lather before getting to work. Confirm prices and exact services offered before you go too far in one of these establishments.

LUXURY HOTELS

What you pay for

The cost of a double room per night, with private bath (except for *ryokan* and hostels), excluding breakfast is shown by the symbols:

S   up to ¥15,000

SS   ¥15,000–¥28,000

SSS over ¥28,000

Tokyo deserves its reputation for high prices, but the top hotels are no more expensive than the equivalent in New York, London, or Frankfurt. Take into account the standard of service, facilities, and impeccable cleanliness, and they might be thought good value. Almost all Japanese hotels provide toothbrushes, toothpaste, a razor and shaving cream, and a cotton *yukata* (robe or pajamas).

AKASAKA PRINCE

The 40-story curved building stands out on its hilltop site, close to Akasaka and a short subway ride from Ginza. Acres of marble, 761 rooms, 12 restaurants, stores, and business services.

✚ H6 ✉ 1-2 Kioi-cho, Chiyoda-ku ☎ 3234–1111; fax 3262–5163 🚇 Nagatacho

ANA HOTEL TOKYO

A 37-story, 903-room block with a sober exterior and lots of marble in the Ark Hills area, between Roppongi and Akasaka. Health club, pool, executive floor, and restaurants.

✚ H7 ✉ 1-12-33 Akasaka, Minato-ku ☎ 3505–1111; fax 3505–1155 🚇 Tameike-sanno

IMPERIAL

A city-within-a-city, in the heart of Ginza and facing Hibiya Park. The 1,059 rooms are beautifully appointed, with superb views from upper floors. Over 20 restaurants, dozens of stores, a health club, and pool.

✚ J6 ✉ 1-1-1 Uchisaiwaicho, Chiyoda-ku ☎ 3504–1251; fax 3581–9146 🚇 Hibiya

NIKKO HOTEL TOKYO

This watefront urban resort, part of the Tokyo Bay area redevelopment (➤ 47), has 453 harbor-view rooms, eight restaurants, two bars, pool.

✚ Off map to south ✉ 1-9-1 Daiba, Minato-ku ☎ 5500–5500; fax 5500–2525 🚇 Daiba (Yurikamome line)

OKURA

Stately and formal, this is one of the first of the postwar grand hotels, with 858 rooms, restaurants, an art gallery, and indoor and outdoor pools.

✚ H7 ✉ 2-10-4 Toranomon, Minato-ku ☎ 3582–0111; fax 3582–3707 🚇 Toranomon

PALACE

Elegant public areas and 393 beautifully appointed guest rooms. A subway stop from Ginza overlooking the moats of the Imperial Palace.

✚ K5 ✉ 1-1-1 Marunouchi, Chiyoda-ku ☎ 3211–5211; fax 3211–6987 🚇 Otemachi

PARK HYATT TOKYO

On the 39th to 52nd floors of a pyramid-topped glass tower at the western edge of Shinjuku. Elegant and spacious, with 178 rooms, 3 restaurants, and a rooftop swimming pool.

✚ C5 ✉ 3-7-1-2 Nishi-Shinjuku, Shinjuku-ku ☎ 5322–1234; fax 5322–1288 🚇 Shinjuku

RENAISSANCE TOKYO

Located in the heart of busy Ginza, this 206-room luxury hotel has two excellent restaurants and a cocktail lounge.

✚ K6 ✉ 6-14-10 Ginza, Chou-ku ☎ 3546–0111; fax 3546–8990 🚇 Yurakucho

WESTIN TOKYO

A stylish hotel with richly decorated public areas and 444 guest rooms, part of an entertainment and shopping complex on the former Sapporo Brewery site.

✚ E10 ✉ Yebisu Garden Place, 1-4-1 Mita, Meguro-ku ☎ 5423–7000; fax 5423–7600 🚇 Ebisu

MID-RANGE HOTELS

ALCYONE

This small, friendly hotel with 74 rooms is one of the cheapest in Ginza.

✚ K6 ✉ 4-14-3 Ginza, Chuo-ku ☎ 3541–3621; fax 3541-3263 🚇 Higashi-Ginza

FAIRMONT

205 rooms in a quiet area on the north side of the Imperial Palace.

✚ J4 ✉ 2-1-17 Kudan-Minami, Chiyoda-ku ☎ 3262–1151; fax 3264–2476 🚇 Kudanshita

GINZA CAPITAL

A basic business hotel with compact rooms, close to Tsukiji subway station, reasonably convenient to Ginza.

✚ L7 ✉ 2-1-4 Tsukiji, Chuo-ku ☎ 3543-7888; fax 3543–7839 🚇 Tsukiji

IBIS

A business hotel with 182 rooms and more than average style close to Roppongi. Busy on weekends.

✚ G7 ✉ 7-14-4 Roppongi, Minato-ku ☎ 3403–4411; fax 3479–0609 🚇 Roppongi

NEW CITY HOTEL

Despite great views over Shinjuku park, this hotel is a bit jaded among its luxury rivals; but it's a good value.

✚ C5 ✉ 31-1-4 Nishi-Shinjuki, Shinjuku-ku ☎ 3375–6511; fax 3375–6535 🚇 JR Shinjuki

ROPPONGI PRINCE

Compact 216-room hotel close to Roppongi. Courtyard with a café and swimming pool.

✚ H7 ✉ 3-2-7 Roppongi, Minato-ku ☎ 3587–1111; fax 3587–0770 🚇 Roppongi

STAR

A small, functional but friendly hotel with 80 rooms, only two-minute walk from Shinjuku Station and the entertainment district.

✚ D4 ✉ 7-10-5 Nishi-Shinjuku, Shinjuku-ku ☎ 3361–1111; fax 3369–4216 🚇 Shinjuku

SUN HOTEL SHINBASHI

A central-area business hotel, three minutes walk from Shinbashi JR or subway stations, one stop away from central Ginza.

✚ J7 ✉ 3-5-2 Shinbashi, Minato-ku ☎ 3591–3351; fax 3592–1977 🚇 Shinbashi

SUN ROUTE SHIBUYA

An efficient, modern 182-room business hotel, one of a Japan-wide chain. Only five minutes walk from Shibuya station.

✚ D8 ✉ 1-11 Nanpeidaimachi, Shibuya-ku ☎ 3464–6411; fax 3464–1678 🚇 Shibuya

TOKYO CITY HOTEL

A typical business hotel in the heart of Nihonbashi, three stops from Ginza by subway.

✚ L5 ✉ 1-5-4 Nihonbashi-honcho, Chuo-ku ☎ 3270–7671; fax 3270–8930 🚇 Mitsukoshi-mae

TOKYO STATION HOTEL

An old-fashioned hotel in part of the historic station building, completed in 1914. Central but with few facilities.

✚ K5 ✉ 1-9-1 Marunouchi, Chiyoda-ku ☎ 3231–2511; fax 3231–3513 🚇 Tokyo

The bare essentials

Most places in the mid-range category are "business hotels," providing a small room and tiny bathroom, telephone, TV, and perhaps an in-house restaurant. The main difference between these and other hotels is location. The relatively high price reflects the cost of land, rents, and labor, not the facilities.

85

BUDGET ACCOMMODATIONS

Your options

Capsule hotels accommodate you in stacked boxes, often likened to coffins. At about 3 feet x 3 feet x 6 feet not for sufferers of claustrophobia. The majority are strictly for men only, mainly those who have partied too long and missed the last train home.

"Love hotels" give couples a chance to be alone together—their success is a direct result of a lack of living space for Tokyoites who often share space with extended families. Rooms are usually rented by the hour, or two; after 10PM an economy all-night rate applies. Love hotels tend to be concentrated in the entertainment districts such as Shibuya, Ikebukuro, East Shinjuku, or Roppongi. Rooms can be elaborately decorated; photos of them are proudly displayed at the entrance.

ASIA CENTER OF JAPAN ($)

A rare budget hotel, with 172 plain, Western-style rooms, some with a private bath. Cafeteria. Reserve well in advance.
✚ H7 ✉ 8-10-32 Akasaka, Minato-ku ☎ 3402–6111; fax 3402–0738 Ⓜ Aoyama-itchome

YMCA ASIA YOUTH CENTER ($$)

Both sexes are welcome. 55 rooms, some with private bath. Seven or eight minutes on foot from Suidobashi or Jinbocho.
✚ J3 ✉ 2-5-5 Saragakucho, Chiyoda-ku ☎ 3233–0611; fax 3233–0633 Ⓜ Suidobashi Ⓜ Jinbocho

YWCA SADOHARA ($$)

Pleasant but very small, this place has a few rooms for couples. A three minutes walk from Ichigaya Station. Reserve ahead.
✚ G4 ✉ 3-1-1 Ichigaya-Sadoharacho, Shinjuku-ku ☎ 3268–7313; fax 3268–4452 Ⓜ Ichigaya

RYOKAN

Traditional Japanese lodging can be expensive and are often reluctant to take foreigners. Rooms normally have *tatami* (mats) and *futon* bedding (a thin mattress and quilt), which is rolled up until evening; a few have Western-style rooms too.

KIMI RYOKAN ($)

This friendly little place with 35 Japanese-style rooms is popular with Westerners and often full. Seven minutes walk northwest of Ikebukuro Station.
✚ Off map ✉ 2-36-8 Ikebukuro, Toshima-ku ☎ 3971–3766; fax 3987–1326 Ⓜ Ikebukuro

SAKURA RYOKAN ($)

Close to Ueno and Asakusa, with 12 Japanese-style and 8 Western- style rooms.
✚ M1 ✉ 2-6-2 Iriya, Taito-ku ☎ 3876–8118; fax 3873–9456 Ⓜ Iriya

SAWANOYA RYOKAN ($)

A modern inn with 12 rooms, close to Ueno Park in the old Yanaka neighborhood.
✚ K1 ✉ 2-3-11 Yanaka, Taito-ku ☎ 3822–2251; fax 3822–2252 Ⓜ Nezu

HOSTELS

Expensive by international standards, hostels are often full. Try to reserve well in advance. There's no age restriction, but if you don't belong to any Youth Hostel Association, you may be charged extra.

TOKYO KOKUSAI YOUTH HOSTEL ($)

Simple dormitory-style accommodations in a modern tower-block. Advance reservations required.
✚ H3 ✉ Central Plaza 18F, 2-1-1 Kaguragashi, Shinjuku-ku ☎ 3235–1107; fax 3267–4000 Ⓜ Iidabashi

TOKYO
travel facts

ARRIVING & DEPARTING

Before you go

- All visitors must have a passport.
- Citizens of the U.S.A., Canada, Netherlands, Australia, and New Zealand may stay 90 days without a visa.
- Citizens of the U.K., Republic of Ireland, and Germany do not need a visa for stays of up to 180 days.
- No inoculations are required.
- Check your insurance coverage before your trip; if necessary, buy a travel policy supplemental.

When to go

- Spring (March–May) brings plum, peach, and cherry blossoms, October through November the golden colors of the fall; but both spring and fall are also peak vacation times for the Japanese.

Climate

- Summers are hot and humid—maximum 90°F
- The rainiest months are June and mid-September to October.
- Spring and fall are warm.
- Winters are very dry and not excessively cold—minumum 37°F. The days are usually brisk and bright.

Arriving by air

- Narita, Tokyo's international airport is 40 miles northeast of the city.
- Airport Limousine and Airport Shuttle coaches run to Tokyo City Air Terminal (TCAT) or to major hotels.
- JR trains connect the airport with Tokyo Station; Keisei Railroad trains link it to Ueno and Higashi-Ginza stations.
- Buses cost about ¥3,000 and take from 70 minutes to 2 hours.
- Train fares cost ¥1,000 – ¥3,000 for the quickest (57 minutes).
- Don't take a taxi: the fare would be at least ¥22,000.
- Tokyo's older airport, Haneda (12 miles south of the city), is used by domestic flights and China Airlines flights to and from Taiwan. A monorail connects it to Hamamatsu-cho Station on the JR Yamanote Line.

Customs regulations

- Duty-free allowances are 200 cigarettes or 50 cigars, 3 x 750ml bottles of liquor, 2oz perfume, ¥200,000 worth of gifts.

Driving

- Congestion, parking difficulties, and Japanese-only signs make it inadvisable for visitors to drive.
- If you must drive, obtain an International Driving Permit before arrival in Japan, and bring your state license as well.
- Traffic keeps to the left. Driving standards are quite good.

ESSENTIAL FACTS

Electricity

- 100V AC, 50Hz. US 110V equipment will operate. Plugs have two flat, parallel pins.

Etiquette

- Japanese custom is to bow when meeting someone. How deeply to bow is a subtle matter of age and status, which, you as a visitor, are not expected to understand. A handshake will be accepted, but an attempt to follow custom will be appreciated.
- When visiting a Japanese home, bring a present, ideally something unusual from your own country, as beautifully wrapped as possible. Do not expect it to be opened in

your presence. You will probably receive something in return, at a later date.

- Shoes must be removed before entering a home, a *ryokan*, many shrine halls, and some restaurants. Slippers are usually provided, but it will save embarrassment if your socks are free from holes.
- Visiting cards are exchanged at every opportunity. If you are on business, take a large supply. They should state your position in your organization. If possible, have a translation in Japanese characters printed on the reverse. Hotels can arrange this quickly. When given a card, study it with interest; do not put it away unread.
- For table etiquette (➤ 65, panel).
- It is not usual to tip in Japan, except for special extra services. A 10–15 percent service charge is added to hotel and some restaurant checks. Porters charge a set fee.

Finding an address

- Few streets have names, and even these are rarely used in addresses. Even taxi drivers have trouble.
- Building numbers generally relate to the order of construction, not to position.
- In a Tokyo address such as 3-10-2 Akasaka (the district), Minato-ku (city ward), 3 is the subdivision or *chome* and 10-2 the building. "F" means floor; ground level is 1F. A map pinpointing the place and related landmarks is essential.

Money matters

- The unit of currency is the yen (¥). Coins in use are ¥1, 5, 10, 50, 100, 500. Banknotes are for ¥1,000, 5,000, and 10,000.
- Traveler's checks in yen may be used instead of cash. Those in other currencies can be changed

at banks or at hotels, where the exchange rate may not be quite as good. A passport is needed.

- Major credit cards are accepted by most hotels, big stores, and many restaurants, but rarely by smaller ones or fast-food outlets. It is still essential, and safe, to carry cash. Telephones and ticket-vending machines take 10, 50, and 100 yen coins.
- ATMs outside banks will take some cards. Check with card issuers to see which are accepted.

National holidays

- If a national holiday falls on a Sunday, the Monday following is a holiday.
- January 1:New Year's Day; 15:Coming of Age Day for 20-year-olds.
- February 1: Foundation Day.
- March 20 or 21: Vernal Equinox Day.
- April 29: Greenery Day.
- May 3: Constitution Day; 4: National Holiday; 5: Children's Day.
- September 15: Respect for the Aged Day; 23 or 24: Fall Equinox Day.
- October 10: Health in Sports Day.
- November 3: Culture Day; 23: Labor Day.
- December 23: Emperor's Birthday.

Opening hours

- Stores: Mon–Sat 10–6, 7 or 8.
- Banks: Mon–Fri 9–3.
- Offices: Mon–Fri 9–5 (businesses work half day on Sat).
- Museums: Tue–Sun 10, 10:30 or 11–4 or 5. (Closed Tue if Mon a national holiday.)

Places of worship

- The following have services in English, call for details:

89

- Roman Catholic: Franciscan Chapel Center ✉ 4-2-37 Roppongi, Minato-ku ☎ 3401–2141
- Protestant: Tokyo Bapist Church ✉ 9-2 Hachiyama-cho, Shibuya-ku ☎ 3461–8425
- Jewish: Jewish Community Center ✉ 3-8-8 Hiroo, Shibuya-ku ☎ 3400–2559
- Islamic: Tokyo Mosque ✉ 1-16 Oyama-cho, Shibuya-ku ☎ 5790–0760
- Interdenominational: Tokyo Union Church ✉ 5-7-7 Jingu-mae, Shibuya-ku ☎ 3400–0047

Restrooms
- Hotels have the Western type; some have heated seats and even an optional "paperless" mode with warm water jets and hot air to clean and dry your underside.
- The Japanese version, in most public lavatories, is at ground level with no seat. You squat over it, facing the flushing handle. Carry your own paper.
- Department stores usually have both versions. Not all public restrooms are segregated.

Student travelers
- An international student card will reduce admission charges at museums and for some other attractions.
- There is a shortage of budget accommodations, but the TCVB helps and publishes lists.

Time differences
- Japan is 13 hours ahead of New York, and 16 hours ahead of San Francisco.

PUBLIC TRANSPORTATION

Buses
- Public buses are slower and more confusing to use than the subway.

Destinations, and information at stops, are usually marked only in Japanese characters.
- Make sure you know the route number, and have your destination written down in Japanese to show people when asking for help.
- On boarding, passengers take a numbered ticket. The fare is shown on an electronic display and paid on leaving the bus.

The subway
- Get a map of the system. Each line is identified by a color, used consistently on maps, signs, and sometimes on the trains too.
- At the station, find the row of ticket machines for that line. Price lists are displayed nearby. If you cannot find one, buy the lowest price ticket and pay any extra at your destination.
- Machines give change.
- Feed the ticket face up into the entry gate and collect it when the machine expels it. Make sure you keep it until the ride is over.
- Follow signs to the line and platform (track) you need, sometimes identified by the last station on the line, so check your map. Stand at the yellow markers, if there are any passengers on the train, wait to one side before boarding.
- At each stop, signs give the station's name and that of the next in Japanese and Roman script.
- At your destination, find an exit directory (a yellow board); note the number of the exit you want before going through the ticket gate. Otherwise you'll walk vast distances and probably get lost.
- Travel light, and at rush hour carry no bags at all. There are many stairs, and long walks to exits or when you are transferring between lines.

Taxis

- The initial charge is high, ¥660 (and 30 percent more from 11PM–5AM) for the first mile and the fare then rises rapidly.
- A red light in the front window indicates that a taxi is available.
- Use the left-hand, curbside door; it opens and closes by remote control. Don't try to do it yourself.
- Drivers will rarely find anything except a big hotel, station, or other landmark from the address alone. It is best to show an area map with your destination marked.
- Pay only the fare on the meter. Tipping is not expected.

Trains

- Within Tokyo, the JR commuter and various private lines operate much the same as the subway.
- The JR Yamanote loop line links important central locations and can be quicker than the subway.
- Tickets are not interchangeable between JR, subway, and private lines.
- The JR has an English-language telephone service ☎ 3423–0111

Where to get maps

- Larger hotels give out excellent city and subway maps; large stations supply subway maps.
- For both leaflets and maps, visit the Tourist Information Centers (TICs) run by JNTO at ✉ Narita Airport Terminal 2, and in the city center at ✚ K6 ✉ Basement of Tokyo International Forum, 3-5-1- Maurunouchi, Chiyada-ku ☎ 3201–3331 🕐 Daily Mon–Fri 9–5, Sat 9–noon 🚇 Yurakucho
- TTIC ✚ K6 ✉ Level 1, Tokyo International Forum, 3-5-1- Maurunouchi, Chiyada-ku ☎ 5221-9084 🕐 Daily 10–6:30 🚇 Yurakucho

Ticket Discounts

- Subway (EIDAN and TOEI lines) and JR one-day tickets allow unlimited travel on their lines that day, but you will rarely justify the expense. A JR Orange Card, EIDAN Metro Card, and TOEI T Card can be used to obtain tickets until the stored value is spent. High denomination cards give a small discount.
- The Japan Rail Pass (for 7, 14, or 21 days unlimited travel on JR trains) is expensive, but can save money on long trips, for example by *shinkansen* ("bullet train") to Kyoto and back. An exchange order has to be purchased outside Japan, and exchanged for the pass itself at a main JR ticket counter. If you do this at Narita Airport on arrival, you can use the pass to travel into the city. It is not valid for the new "Nozomi" super express train.

MEDIA & COMMUNICATIONS

International newsdealers

- A full range of foreign magazines is stocked at newsstands in big hotels and major railroad stations, and in large bookstores (► 76).

Listings magazines

- The monthly *Tokyo Journal* has full listings of exhibitions, flea markets, services, and entertainment. Restaurant, club, and bar reviews may be biased in favor of advertisers.
- *City Life News Tokyo* (monthly), *Tokyo Notice Board*, and *Tokyo Weekender* (with Saturday's *Daily Yomiuri*) carry articles on the Tokyo scene.

Newspapers

- There are four English-language translations of the main Japanese dailies: the *Japan Times*, *Daily*

91

Yomiuri, Mainichi Daily News, and *Asahi Evening News*.

- The *International Herald Tribune*, *Financial Times*, and *Asian Wall Street Journal* are also available on the day of publication.

Post offices

- Hotel desks are the most convenient place to mail letters and cards. They have stamps and are familiar with postal rates.
- Go to post offices only to send heavy packages or registered mail. Staff can read Roman script.
- Post offices open Mon–Fri 9–5.
- 24-hour post office: Tokyo International Post Office ✉ **2-3-3 Otemachi, Chiyoda-ku**

Radio

- FM radio stations broadcast Western and Japanese classical, popular, and rock music.
- The U.S. armed services have a general information and entertainment AM radio station: Far East Network (FEN) 810 Hz.

Television

- The domestic TV channels have little to interest visitors, except perhaps the news and weather in simultaneous English translation (available at the push of a button on many sets), and sport.
- Major hotels have satellite channels including news in English on CNN and BBC World.

Telephones

- Coin- and card-operated phones are prevalent. Local calls cost ¥10 per minute. ¥500 or ¥1,000 cards are sold at hotels, airports, station kiosks, and machines near phones.
- Make international direct-dial calls from gray and green phones with a gold front panel, card phones, or phones marked

"international." Use only ¥100 coins, or cards. Several companies compete, each having its own international access code. Dial 001(for KDD), 0041 (ITJ) or 0061 (IDC), followed by the country code, area code (omit any initial 0), and number. The calling card codes of other international companies can also be used. MCI ☎ **0039–121 or 0066–55–121;** AT&T ☎ **0039–111 or 0066–55–111**

- Direct dialing from hotel rooms is expensive.
- Dial 0051 for person-to-person and collect (reverse charge) calls, and 0057 (toll-free) for information.
- Mobile phones from other countries are not compatible with Japanese networks.

EMERGENCIES

Emergency phone numbers

- Police ☎ 110
- Fire and Ambulance ☎ 119
- Emergency numbers are toll-free. On pay phones, push the red button first.
- There are police boxes (*koban*) on many street corners and resident police in every little district. They usually speak only Japanese.

Embassies

- Australia ✉ **2-1-14 Mita, Minato-ku, Tokyo 108** ☎ **5232–4111**
- Canada ✉ **7-3-38 Akasaka, Minato-ku, Tokyo 107** ☎ **3412–6200**
- Germany ✉ **4-5-10 Minami-azabu, Minato-ku, 106** ☎ **3473–0151**
- Netherlands ✉ **3-6-3 Shiba-koen, Minato-ku, 10** ☎ **5401–0411**
- New Zealand ✉ **20-40 Kamiyama-cho, Shibuya-ku, Tokyo 150** ☎ **3467–2271**
- U.K. ✉ **1 Ichiban-cho, Chiyoda-ku, Tokyo 102** ☎ **3265–6340**
- U.S.A. ✉ **1-10-5 Akasaka, Minato-ku, Tokyo 107** ☎ **3224–5000**

Lost and found

- Trains: Teito (EIDAN) subway lines ☎ 3834–5577; TOEI lines: ☎ 3815–7229; JR trains ☎ 3231–1880 (Tokyo Station) ☎ 3841–8069 (Ueno Station)
- Taxis: ☎ 3648–0300
- Buses: ☎ 3818–5760

Medical treatment

- Standards are high, and so are costs.
- Your embassy can recommend hospitals with some doctors who speak English.

Medication

- For prescription and non-pre-scription medication, when you need an English speaker: American Pharmacy ✚ K6 ✉ Hibiya Park Building 1-8-1 Yurakucho, Chiyodu-ku ☎ 3271–4034 🕙 Mon–Sat 9–8; Sun 10–6:30 🚇 Ginza

Sensible precautions

- Tokyo is the safest of the world's big cities to walk around. Even in the raunchier areas, such as Kabukicho, you need not be too apprehensive: when the locals drink too much, they are rarely aggressive.
- Use hotel safes for storing large sums of money.
- Streets and subways are safe, but always exercise the same precautions as in any city when walking at night.

LANGUAGE

- Romanized versions of Japanese words are more or less phonetic, so say the words as written.
- Give all syllables equal weight, except: "u" at the end of a word, which is hardly sounded at all; "i" in the middle of a word, which is skipped over, as in mash'te

for -mashite.
- E sounds like "eh" in ten; g is generally hard, as in go.
- Two adjoining consonants are sounded separately.
- A dash over a vowel lengthens the vowel sound.
- Family names are now usually written second.

Useful words & phrases

How do you do? Hajime-mashite?
Good morning Ohayo gozai-masu
Good afternoon Kon-nichi-wa
Good evening Konban-wa
Good night Oyasumi-nasai
Goodbye Sayo-nara
Mr., Mrs., Miss, Ms. -san (suffix to family name, or given name of friends)
Thank you Domo/arigato
Don't mention it Do itashi-mashite
Excuse me, sorry Sumi-masen
Please (when offering) Dozo
Please (when asking) Kudasai
Hello (telepone) Moshi-moshi
Yes Hai
Do you understand? Wakari-masu-ka?
Do you speak English? Eigo o hanashi-masu-ka?
I don't understand Japanese Nihon-go ga wakari-masen
How much is it? Ikura desu-ka?
Where is ...? ... wa doko desu-ka?
...train station ...eki
... hotel ... hoteru
left/right hidari/migi
north/south kita/minami
east/west higashi/nishi

Numbers

1	ichi	9	kyu (or ku)
2	ni	10	ju (or to)
3	san	11	ju-ichi
4	shi (or yon)	20	ni-ju
5	go	30	san-ju
6	roku	40	yon-ju
7	nana (or shichi)	100	hya-ku
8	hachi	1,000	sen

INDEX

Citypack
Tokyo

AUTHOR *Martin Gostelow*
THIRD EDITION UPDATED BY *Rod Ritchie and Julia Walkden*
CARTOGRAPHY *The Automobile Association*
RV Reise- und Verkehrsverlag
MANAGING EDITOR *Hilary Weston*
COVER DESIGN *Fabrizio La Rocca, Tigist Getachew*
COVER PICTURES *AA Photo Library*

ISBN 679–00694–X
Third Edition

Acknowledgments

The Automobile Association wishes to thank the following photographers, associations,
and libraries for their assistance in the preparation of this book: M. Gostelow 5b, 16, 20, 35,
60, 63b; Japanese National Tourist Organization 62; National Museum of Modern Art 37b;
Ota Memorial Museum of Art 52; Rex Features Ltd 9, 12; Spectrum Colour Library 1, 6, 7,
13a, 13b, 19, 21, 25a, 26, 28a, 30a, 30b, 36, 38a, 39, 40b, 41, 49b, 51a, 55, 63a; Suntory
Museum 53; Tokyo Convention & Visitors Bureau 32, 34b, 47, 48, 54; Tokyo National
Museum 25b; Zefa Pictures Ltd 2, 5a, 87a. All remaining pictures are held in the
Association's own library (AA Photo Library) and were taken by J. Holmes, with the
exception of 27a, 46, 47, 49a, 59, which were taken by D. Corrance, and 29a, 29b, 37a, 42b,
87b, which were taken by R. T. Alford.

Important tip

Time inevitably brings changes, so always confirm prices, travel facts, and other perishable
information when it matters. Although Fodor's cannot accept responsibility for errors, you can
use this guide in the confidence that we have taken every care to ensure its accuracy.

Special sales

Fodor's Travel Publications are available at special discounts for bulk purchases
(100 copies or more) for sales promotions or premiums. Special editions, including
personalized covers, excerpts of existing guides, and corporate imprints, can be created
in large quantities for special needs. For more information contact your local bookseller
or write to Special Marketing, Fodor's Travel Publications, 280 Park Avenue, New York,
NY 10017. Inquiries from Canada should be directed to your local Canadian bookseller
or sent to Random House of Canada, Ltd., Marketing Department, 2775 Matheson
Blvd. East, Mississauga, Ontario L4W 4P7.

Color separation by Daylight Colour Art Pte Ltd, Singapore
Manufactured by Dai Nippon Printing Co. (Hong Kong) Ltd
10 9 8 7 6 5 4 3 2 1

Titles in the Citypack series

- ● Amsterdam ● Barcelona ● Beijing ● Berlin ● Boston ● Brussels & Bruges ●
- ● Chicago ● Dublin ● Florence ● Hong Kong ● Lisbon ● London ● Los Angeles ●
- ● Madrid ● Melbourne ● Miami ● Montreal ● Munich ● New York ● Paris ●
- ● Prague ● Rome ● San Francisco ● Seattle ● Shanghai ● Sydney ● Tokyo ●
- ● Toronto ● Venice ● Vienna ● Washington, D.C. ●